SCOTTISH RO

To

JEAN *and* POPSY

Their smiles were Irish
but their roots were Scottish

SCOTTISH ROOTS

A step-by-step guide
for ancestor-hunters
in Scotland and Overseas

ALWYN JAMES

MACDONALD PUBLISHERS
Loanhead, Midlothian

ISBN 0 904265 45 5 *cased*
0 904265 46 3 *limp*

Published by
Macdonald Publishers
Loanhead, Midlothian EH20 9SY

First published March 1981
Reprinted October 1981
2nd Reprint March 1983
3rd Reprint August 1984
4th Reprint October 1985
5th Reprint October 1986

Printed in Scotland by
Macdonald Printers (Edinburgh) Limited
Edgefield Road, Loanhead, Midlothian EH20 9SY

Contents

Introduction

WHEN a Welshman married to an Irish girl lands up writing a book on how to trace your Scottish ancestors, he owes his readers something of an explanation.

I came to Edinburgh in April 1970, along with my Dublin wife, four sons born in London, a degree from an English university and a Welsh birth certificate. These, it appeared, qualified me to edit the business and political magazine *Scotland*. This I dutifully did for the next three-and-a-half years. And that was time enough to get me (and the rest of the family) firmly hooked on Scotland, its history and people, its politics and potential, its culture and even its rugby. (I might add that I had already appreciated its one export, whisky, and never got to grips with its other, golf).

When my wife, Jean, with green eyes and Irish lilt, announced that her grandfather was Scottish, we sniffed some real tartan roots and Jean set off in what little spare time she had (in between looking after me and the ravenous boys) to see what could be found in the Scottish records. She seemed to be going well until she discovered she had got her grandfather's name wrong and was barking up the wrong family tree.

I started work as a freelance, Jean went out to work and I had in the early months a lot of what is euphemistically called "thinking time" on my hands.

I decided to take up where Jean had left off (we had by then discovered the real Christian name of her grandfather) and, encouraged by the benefit of an unusual Scottish name (you don't find a Robert Balbirnie on every street corner), plunged into the depths of New Register House. Within hours I had contracted that appalling and increasingly common disease of ancestor-hunting, a disease for which there is no known cure.

Ancestor-hunting, even in this form, one step removed from my own family, has everything: the magnetism of the puzzle, the thrill of the chase, the challenge of the unknown—and the very real sense of exploring territory which has not been surveyed and measured, logged and plotted by all and sundry. Add to this the fact that it is your own ancestors you are identifying and learning about and you will get an inkling of the power of the addiction.

Now is of course the age of the ancestor-hunter. For decades, people had ceased to bother about their forebears—especially in the teeming urban centres—and I think I was perhaps typical of my generation in not being able to go back beyond my grandparents. Searching for forebears had been the preserve of those whose families had done great or dastardly deeds, had signed treaties or led armies. Today, there is an intrinsic interest in roots, no matter how lowly or unsung the people involved.

There is still a thrill to be got from finding someone out of the ordinary in your family tree. (I have not yet managed to unearth such a one, although I get some pleasure from seeing snooker star Ray Reardon dangling from one of the lower branches). But there is now no longer the quest for a rightful title or desire to link on to the aristocracy in genealogical endeavour; it is a matter of roots for roots' sake.

If *now* is the time to be looking for ancestors, then Scotland is the place. Having done (and been deterred from pursuing) a little family research on my Welsh roots, I had had some experience of the system south of Hadrian's Wall—slow, frustrating and expensive.

Seeing just what was available in Scotland opened my eyes to the tremendous advantages Scots and the descendants of Scots have over their neighbours in the British Isles. The country has a rich and colourful past by any standards and few countries if any can compare with Scotland's past two hundred and fifty years, precisely the period most of you are going to be concerned with in your ancestor-hunting.

What is truly staggering is the extent to which this tapestry of politics and industry, art and culture, invention and community, is an open book to those who want to find out just what their ancestors were doing when Scotland was passing through those two and half momentous centuries.

This book is an attempt to show what can be achieved by Scots who have not yet become aware of the rich legacy of records and documents which can allow even people from the humblest origins to span those centuries.

It is not intended to provide the exhaustive and definitive guide to all the many sources. A number of extremely good books already perform that function. It will, I hope, give enough of the bald and basic facts—what information exists, where it is kept, how you can get hold of it, what you will find when you see it, how to log the information—to make you feel at home in the environment of papers and documents, indexes and official records, to encourage you to make a serious (but not necessarily solemn) search for the people who have gone into the manufacture of that unique product—YOU.

Acknowledgments

As THE dedication and introduction stress, the main debt is to my wife Jean, for her consideration in having only three of her grandparents Irish, and for getting me started.

I would also like to thank:

The Royal Bank for permission to use the material and case histories which appeared originally in my series "McRoots" in the staff newspaper *Countertalk*.

Bob Leitch and Pauline Brydon for the patience and good humour they displayed as my "guinea-pigs" in those case-histories.

The staff of New Register House for the many hours of cheerful and helpful co-operation I received over the years. The Repository Assistants deserve the lion's share of that gratitude in view of the many volumes they have lifted and stairs they have trudged on my behalf.

Alan Seaton for the composition of the family tree on pages 88-9.

John Hutchison and Moira Campbell of the Scottish Tourist Board for their help on the folk museums.

The Church of Scotland for permission to reproduce items from the Old Parochial Records.

Dr Ian Grant at New Register House for his advice and guidance.

Glasgow District Council for the photograph on page 111 of the magnificent new extension to the Mitchell Library.

The documents reproduced between pages 35 and 58 are Crown copyright and are reproduced with the approval of the Registrar-General for Scotland and the permission of the Controller of Her Majesty's Stationery Office.

BASE ONE

Genealogy begins at home

The work you can get down to at home straightaway can simplify your ancestor-hunting later on

> Tom was always singing and when he was older he used to go for voice training and started singing operatic pieces. There used to be a chip cart coming round in the evenings. The man driving and serving was an Italian. We all looked forward to a ½d bag of chips which was delicious, but Tom was more concerned with trying out his Italian on the man and following his cart all around the town.

Genealogy, like charity, begins at home—and the information above, referring to the pursuits of an uncle of mine before the 1914-18 War, came as the result of the work I did on building up a family history not in some large repository of documents but at home. And you too can get down to the business of ancestor-hunting immediately, without waiting for your next trip to Edinburgh or even your next visit to Scotland.

The work you can do at home is, moreover, just as important as any of the pouring over records or reference books in the libraries or record offices where you will be spending much of your time later in the quest. Indeed, these first few steps can help clarify in your mind just what it is you are tackling, can set patterns for your later work (important when the volume of information gets greater and might

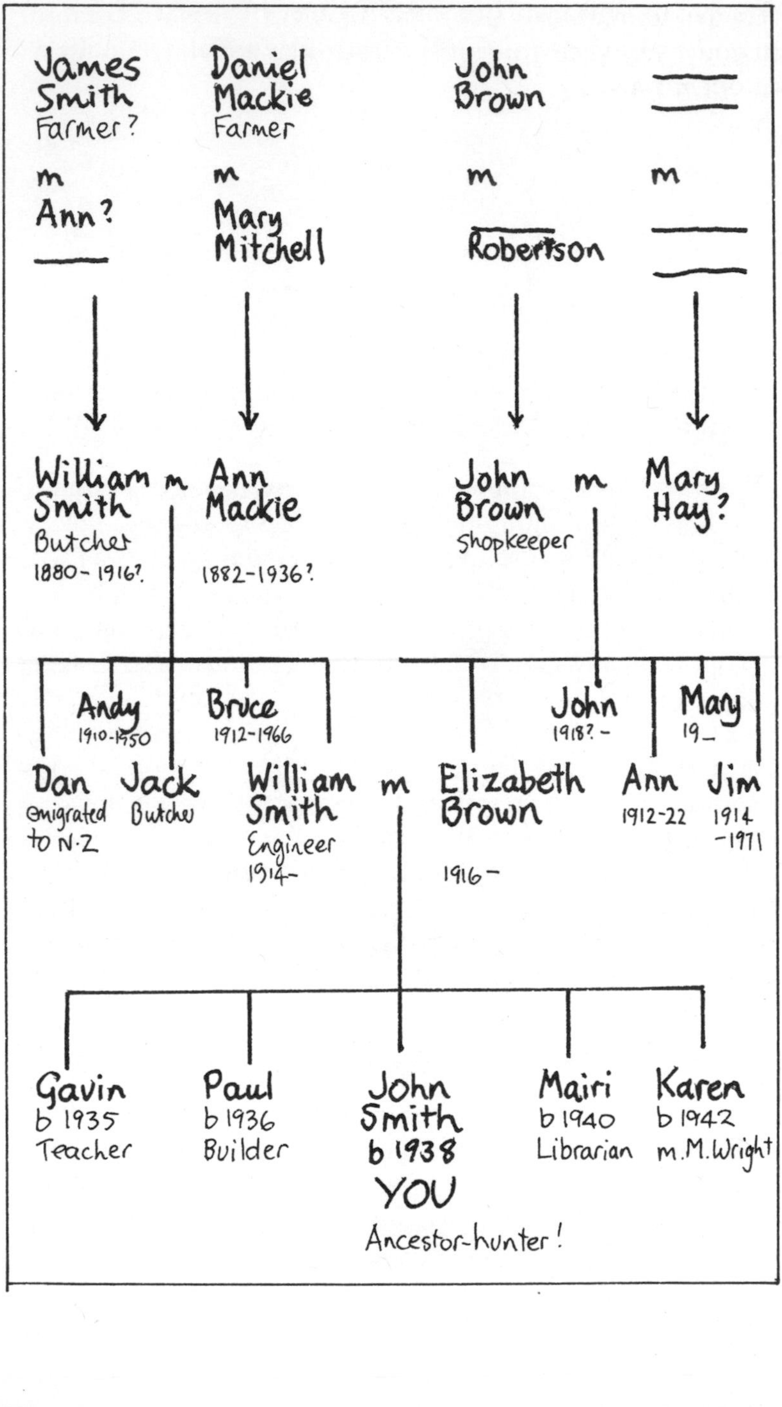
James Smith
Farmer?
m
Ann?
Daniel Mackie
Farmer
m
Mary Mitchell
John Brown
m
Robertson
m
William Smith
Butcher
1880–1916?
m
Ann Mackie
1882–1936?
John Brown
Shopkeeper
m
Mary Hay?
Andy
1910–1950
Bruce
1912–1966
John
1918? –
Mary
19_
Dan
emigrated to N.Z
Jack
Butcher
William Smith
Engineer
1914–
m
Elizabeth Brown
1916–
Ann
1912–22
Jim
1914 –1971
Gavin
b 1935
Teacher
Paul
b 1936
Builder
John Smith
b 1938
YOU
Ancestor-hunter!
Mairi
b 1940
Librarian
Karen
b 1942
m. M. Wright

threaten to intimidate you), and can help you make the most of your time when you come face-to-face with large numbers of documents.

FIRST STEP

Take a sheet of paper, not too mean in size—and you can get started right away on that intriguing jig-saw of a hobby where you start with one little piece (yourself) and from that centre-point work outwards in ever increasing circles, each step giving you more and more pieces to look for, occasionally resulting in a dead-end but never reaching the borders of the infinite picture you are constructing.

Write down your own name and work upwards in a simple little line chart of parents, grandparents and even have a bash at your great-grandparents. You should end up with something like the diagram shown alongside.

Now try filling in a few dates of births and marriages and deaths. And when you've done that, how about some addresses and occupations.

When you've got into the swing of things, start branching out into aunts and uncles, brothers and sisters and see just how far you can get. You will probably land up with a very congested network.

You may be an exception to the general rule but I'll assume for the moment that you are not and that four basic comments can apply to your chart:

1. You have lots of names in your own generation, not so many in your parents' generation "band" and not many at all in your grandparents' band.
2. You won't go back very far beyond your grandparents.
3. Your dates and addresses will be very vague.
4. You will have surprised yourself at the gaps as far as such things as your grandmother's maiden name are concerned.

For all those limitations, the chart will clearly set the targets for your work of ancestor-hunting—to fill in those gaps, clarify those dates, and extend the whole chart back as far beyond your grandparents as possible. And when you realise the pace at which those ancestors multiply—four grandparents, eight great-grandparents, 16 great-great-grandparents etc.—you will see that, even discounting the brothers and sisters of all those people, there are a lot of ancestors up there waiting to be discovered. You should, for example, have little difficulty in getting back to 1800—and at that date there may very well have been 64 people from whom you can claim direct descent!

But patience, let us get back to basics.

Having exhausted your own fund of knowledge, it is time to get in touch with those relatives who can add to your list, tell you that Uncle Jack was a railwayman, that his sister went to New Zealand, that Ned was married twice and what-have-you. And, perhaps, even extend your chart into new generation bands.

Some of those relatives will be living near at hand: go and talk to them. Some will be a bus-ride away: go and visit them. Some will be out of reach as far as a visit is concerned: write to them.

There is no way in which I can overemphasise the importance of getting down to these tasks as soon as possible. Aunt Aggie's birth certificate will be available for study for years to come; Aunt Aggie may not.

FACE TO FACE

You will find out from the start that diplomacy and tact are useful attributes to the genealogist—and that shyness or reticence are distinct handicaps. At this stage, some books dwell on the problems of getting information from elderly relatives. These difficulties are, to a large extent, imaginary, most older folk relishing the chance to talk about Auld Lang Syne, long-dead relatives and distant kinsmen!

In essence, you are looking for three distinct types of information:

1. Names and places

You will be keen to add to the information that you were trying to piece together in your first tentative chart—who married whom, what they did, how many children they had, what they worked at. Older relatives will, by the very nature of things, be strong in those bands where you have been weak.

2. Documents and photographs

Over the years, your family, just like any other, must have acquired at various "points" (*i.e.* members) letters, diaries, photographs, bank books, life assurance policies, deeds, and what have you. The relatives you are going to contact may be able to help you locate these. They may know where the family bible went, who got the only photograph of great-uncle George in his army uniform, where Billy's letters from Ypres landed up.

3. Reminiscences

Arguably, the most important of these three is the story of the family as seen by any older relative. And that person doesn't have to be a 90-year-old to make his or her story worth listening to. I make no apology for repeating that in this case, as to a lesser extent in the first two types, there is an immediacy in the matter. The sooner you start getting in touch, the better.

THE VISIT

There are many roles which the ancestor-seeker is called upon to play in his hobby. In the business of "pumping" relatives, it is necessary to acquire at some speed the skills of the journalist. The task is eased in most cases by the willingness, if not eagerness, of most elderly relatives to respond to any sign of interest from the younger generation! Again, you will, from the tips above and from your own "tree" sketch, have a clear idea of just what it is you are looking for. The taking of notes does, however, pose a problem to anyone not used to this deceptively difficult task. Technology has come to your aid in the form of the compact, modern cassette recorder. Remember: you are aiming to record a conversation, not a concert, and quality of sound is less important than a simple, unobtrusive machine that will not put off the person whose reminiscences you are taping. For the same reason, go for the long-playing tapes that will cut down the need to interrupt a flow of words to change a tape.

If at all possible, get hold of a tape-recorder rather than plump for note-taking; unless you are fast and experienced, this is a bit of a gamble, as most of us can keep up with even moderate conversation only with difficulty. And there is nothing more offputting to the elderly aunt in full flow than to have you saying "How do you spell that?", "Did you say 1944?" or "Could you stop a moment while I get that down?"

If you have to take notes, minimise the problems by realising that it is only the key points you want to record. In this case, as soon as you get home, go over the notes, expanding and clarifying any points while your recollection of the conversion is still fresh.

So off we go. Whether you are using tape-recorder or notes (or indeed a combination of both), it is best to get the conversation under way without either. Your own efforts at compiling a family tree will provide a good starting-off point and, as most people love to be able to add to or correct someone else's work, this should get your aged relative going.

The information which starts to flow will provide a good and natural link with your request to produce notebook and/or tape-recorder, and with a bit of luck Aunt Ethel or Uncle Jimmie will be in full swing and in no mood to be intimidated by either. (Incidentally, with mention of Aunt and Uncle, it is worth underlining here the benefits of getting *two* relatives together for the interview. You'll be surprised at the way in which the two will spark off lines of thought one with another. The disadvantages—mainly difficulty in keeping control of the conversation—are more than outweighed by the very real advantages which emerge).

1. Names and places

Start your recorder (or head the page of your notebook) with the date, place and the people involved in the conversation. Concentrate on the top end of your own chart and, when someone's name crops up, get the information flowing with such queries as "Where did he live?", "What did he do?", "Whom did he marry?" or "Did they have any children?"

There are a few points to try and remember during this section of the interview:

- Try and establish dates—and, if there is difficulty in getting these with any degree of accuracy, try at least to relate events in your family not only to obvious "landmarks," such as the Wars or the Coronation, but also to each other, such as "Did that happen after they moved to Carlisle?" or "Was Donald born at that point?"

- In particular, try and get some semblance of order in the people mentioned. Your elderly relative will, I have found, happily reel off aunts and uncles and cousins, but to make sense out of this at a later stage it would help to know the answers to such questions as "Who was the youngest sister?", "Was she older than you?"

- When it comes to a question of the jobs of some of the people, try and find out who they worked for, rather than just the fact that Uncle Jimmie was a carpenter. Was he a master-carpenter? Did he run his own business? Did he work for someone else? If someone was in the army, which regiment? If someone was a teacher, at which school? A railway worker, on which line?

Wedding photographs are especially fruitful. When you come across one, get an elderly relative to help you go systematically through the names and faces. Don't forget to ask about the relatives you think should have been in the group and weren't: I was rewarded with an interesting anecdote when I asked my father why Uncle Tom was nowhere to be seen in this 1922 wedding group.

- One aspect of occupation which is often neglected on such records as marriage entries is the question of what the young women did. Once married, the role of a housewife took up most of a woman's time and working wives were not as common as today, but before marriage the woman might be working in a shop or a mill—and your elderly relative might remember.

2. Documents and photographs

I mentioned earlier that your family must have acquired over the years a host of bits of paper which you would like to get your hands on. Equally certainly, a huge proportion of these will have been jettisoned, lost or destroyed. But there will undoubtedly be some around somewhere—and your aged relative might be able to help locate them. It is not enough to ask bluntly, "Where are the family papers?" Try going through a list of the sort of things you are looking for—and don't be self-conscious about producing an actual check-list to read out. It shows you are in earnest—and might also jog the memory when specific items are mentioned. Here is the sort of check-list you may like to start with:

- Diaries, letters, notebooks—the real cream—and don't be too disappointed if you don't find any!

- Copies of Birth, Marriage and Death Certificates—the more you can collect now the fewer you have to hunt for in the official files.

- Wills, deeds, insurance policies.

- Photographs—again real gems. In particular, look for family groupings. A wedding photograph, for example, is ideal, especially if you can find relatives to name the people shown.

- Books owned by earlier relatives—and it is not just the family Bible which is likely to contain information on the fly-leaf; many old books will contain addresses, perhaps a forgotten maiden name. (Since starting to type this chapter, I have been shown a prayerbook by my sister-in-law which belonged to her grandmother. It contained: evidence of a previous marriage, the surname on the fly-leaf being neither the maiden name nor the only name we knew for the lady, an address and a date, and five cuttings from newspaper relating to deaths of friends and relatives).

- Books or articles written by relatives even if not related to family matters.

- Details of any land owned or court cases involving relatives—which will lead you to records and documents held by specific offices.

- Any information regarding schools or universities attended, army or navy service—again helping you move on to outside sources of documentation.

- Any other work similar to one you are attempting to produce. Don't be put off if you are told that Old Jake did all this before. Even if you manage to get hold of his records, you can bet that he had still left plenty for you to do!

3. Reminiscences

Talk to anyone who has got hooked on this ancestor-hunting and you'll find that he or she will have a wistful regret at not having spoken to (or even listened to) now long-dead relatives who had so much to tell about the family roots. Get down to the real task of doing what you can with the relatives who are available, especially in this matter of memories. "Old men forget," said the English Bard, but it is equally true that they remember—and that is what you are interested in.

Once again, it is important in your role of catalyst to be specific. Don't just ask "What do you remember of your childhood?" Try precise triggers such as "Where did you go to school?", "How did you get there?", "What do you remember about your teachers?", "Your friends?" Find out about the home and the family: "How many rooms did you have?'', ''Who slept where?'', ''What do you remember most about your brothers and sisters as children?'', ''Where did you go on your holidays?'' (This is often a surprisingly fruitful source of information, as in the days before Benidorm and Butlin's children usually travelled to relatives for their holidays, and this will even open up some branches which had not emerged earlier in the conversation).

In the long run, the style of the interview will depend to a large extent more on the character of you and your relative rather than on these notes—but they will help you discipline your approach.

TACKLING DISTANT RELATIVES

The problem of the distant relative (and that refers to geography rather than relationship or temperament!) is a formidable one. It is impossible to get the rapport and feed-back of a face-to-face chat, but it *is* possible to extract a great deal of information by post. Again you are dealing with those three basic areas of investigation and again you should try and tackle all of them precisely and effectively.

1. Send your own efforts at a chart along. Ask if your relative can add any names, dates, places, occupations.
2. Send along your check-list of documents and photographs. (If you locate a source of family photographs, your relative may very well be reluctant to commit them to you and the postman—so think about footing the bill for the neighbourhood photographer to copy them).
3. Send along blank sheets of paper with a simple, single reminiscence question at the top: ''What do you remember about your school?'', ''Your Church?'', ''Your house?'', ''Your brothers?'', ''Your sisters?'',''Your aunts?'', ''Your uncles?'' Even be specific enough to name individuals. One such sheet I sent to an eighty-four-year-old aunt produced the information given at the

NAME James Dundas BALBIRNIE

~~BIRTH~~/BAPTISM REGISTRATION Edinburgh 1822

Date and place 15 October 1822 - College Parish
Father William Balbirnie, copper engraver
Mother Catherine Johnstone
Reported by/Witnesses

~~MARRIAGE~~/BANNS REGISTRATION Edinburgh 1846

Date and place Banns 7 June 1846
Address 275 High Street, Edinburgh
Age and occupation
Parents
SPOUSE Isabella McFARLANE
Witnesses

DEATH REGISTRATION 1871 Newington 189

Date and place 15 S. Clerk St, Edin. 23 March 1871
Cause of death Concussion of the Brain
Age and occupation 49, manager, map engraving
Burial details
Reported by William Balbirnie son.
Parents William Balbirnie, copper engraver. Catherine J.

CHILDREN

William	Thomas	Janet Catherine
Robert	John Hay	
Alexander	James	

CENSUS DETAILS

1841	150 High St, Edin	1871	[15 S. Clerk St]
1851	33 Arthur St.	1881	
1861	17 Arthur St	1891	

GENERATION BAND 5

beginning of this chapter. And that is a piece of information which would never emerge from the records of births, marriages and deaths.

Finally, include a stamped addressed envelope. It is surprising just how effective it can be to make a reply as simple as possible, especially to older people who may require a long walk to get an envelope or stamp. (Those blank sheets with headings also help out here).

You are now well on the way to an attack on the massive stores of documents and records, but there is still much that can be done at home to prepare for and simplify that project.

PREPARING TO RECEIVE INFORMATION

For many people, the study of documents and the making of notes is a new and daunting prospect. The aim of this book is in fact to help you cope with the mass of facts and dates which will soon be coming your way—by showing you exactly what you can expect, what you should look for and how you should handle the information you collect.

There is no one answer to how you should log the results of your research, but here are two suggestions.

In his very fine booklet, *Introducing Scottish Genealogical Research,* Donald Whyte illustrates a *family group sheet* in which, as the name suggests, the unit is the family, with husband and wife (with names of their parents) fully detailed along with all children. This gives a very clear picture of all groupings and in particular will show at a glance the name patterns which, as I outline in Appendix II, were a helpful and widespread feature of Scottish families during the period we shall be studying.

I, alas, have got firmly hooked on the use of *individual* sheets in which a sheet is devoted to a single person rather than to a family group. An example of the sheet is shown alongside.

The advantages are that the amount of space given allows you to include full details of jobs, addresses and ancillary but often helpful details such as witnesses, who was the informant (*i.e.* who provided the information to the registrar), causes of death and references to the Census returns, and it still leaves room for the inevitable marginal notes, referring for example to wills, directory entries or legal cases. The generation band is clearly marked on each sheet (counting yourself as 1, your parents as 2, your grand-parents as 3 etc.) and sheets can, at any stage, be arranged together into family groupings as required.

No matter which of these approaches you go for, the sheets can be provided in quantity by typing or neatly drawing out the form on to an A4 sheet of paper (297 × 210 mm, the standard business letter size) and having this duplicated at any of the many copy-service centres which are available in most towns. If there is any problem here, a local business firm might very well do the job for you at a reasonable charge. Fifty *family* sheets would keep you busy for a while, the *individual* sheets clearly needing more, perhaps as many as 200.

These sheets will form the basis of your master records and should be kept at home to receive the information you collect from personal and official records.

NOTEPADS AT THE READY

The first big target will be the records of Births, Marriages and Deaths for Scotland from 1855 to the present day—and this will be tackled in some detail in the next chapter. One thing which you can do at home in advance of your visit to New Register House is to prepare the notebooks which you will use there. Again the question of note-taking is a very personal one—and you will see every type of notebook being used, from large and voluminous pads to tiny wallet-size ring-books. . . . One thing is certain—you must turn up with a substantial amount of paper to cope with the information.

I prefer the standard journalist/shorthand ring notebook. I start off with three—one for Births, one for Marriages and one for Deaths. This slight extravagance makes it possible to do, in advance, a lot of the writing which would otherwise take up valuable time in amongst the registers. Alternatively, you can divide the book into three—the first part for Births, the second for Marriages and the third for Deaths.

At home, you can fill in the headings of a number of pages, at the time itemising the sort of information which you wish to transcribe from the records. The sheets might be drawn up as illustrated. (Note: at this stage you can use ink for the headings, but when it comes to transcribing from the actual records you *must* use a pencil; the risk of permanent deface- ment from leaking fountain pens or ball-points is too great).

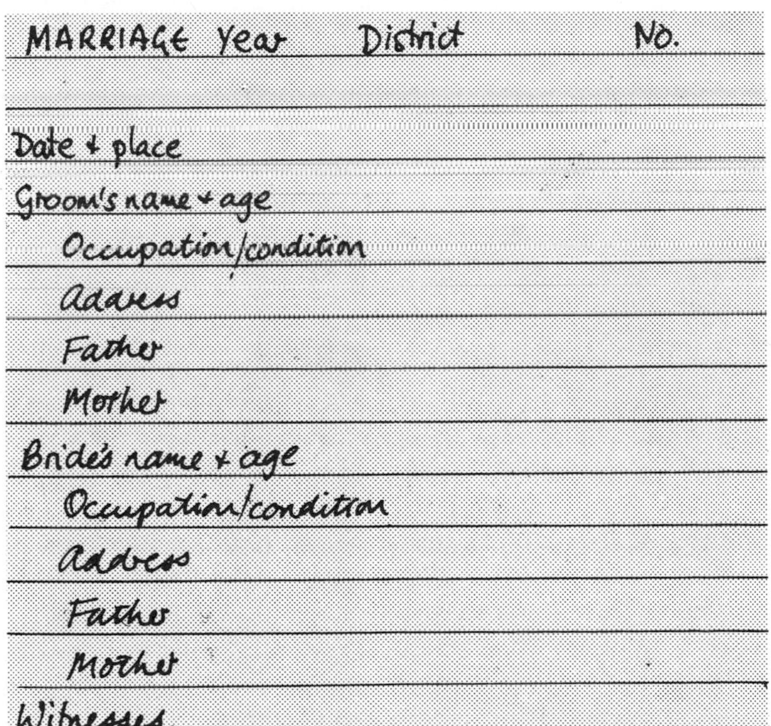

MARRIAGE Year District No.
Date + place
Groom's name + age
Occupation/condition
Address
Father
Mother
Bride's name + age
Occupation/condition
Address
Father
Mother
Witnesses.

I shall deal with those headings when we come to look at the records of Births, Marriages and Deaths in the next chapter, but at this stage you can see that to have the skeleton in front of you not only makes it easier to concentrate on the essentials when you are studying the actual entries but also reduces the possibility of your missing out an essential item.

A BOOK AND A MAP

One final area in which you can get down to valuable work at home is swotting up the background. At this stage, you may not know exactly which part of Scotland you are going to be concentrating on, but as soon as the search becomes more localised it is important, *especially in the rural areas,* to get hold of a good Ordnance Survey map of the area. These often include names of old places, forgotten places, small places, which it would otherwise be difficult to relate to each other. It will also help you to track down addresses which you will be coming across in the records. In the case of the cities, a good street map would be helpful. While ideally an old map is to be preferred, it is surprising how many modern street maps of Scottish towns can prove helpful in locating nineteenth-century addresses.

The map or maps will provide you with valuable geographical information; you will also need some historical background as your search progresses. Here I have no hesitation in recommending a single book, Professor T. C. Smout's *A History of the Scottish People, 1560-1830,* a superb work on the people of Scotland, clearly describing the social context in which your ancestors lived, whether they were miners or lawyers, weavers or landowners, farmers or doctors. Superb illustrations and the rare combination of learning and style make this an ideal book for the would-be ancestor-hunter, whether he is a devoted addict of historical writing or someone coming to the field as a novice. And the book is now even available in paper-back, thanks to Fontana.

This is also the time to make contact with the Federation of Family History Society. See Appendix VII.

BASE TWO

New Register House, Edinburgh

The General Register Office for Scotland— 125 years of Births, Marriages and Deaths, returns from six censuses, records from more than 900 parishes

AT THE east end of Princes Street, modestly peeping from behind the contrasting shoulders of Woolworths and Register House, lies New Register House, the headquarters of the Registrar-General for Scotland. There, under one roof or perhaps dome to be more precise, lies the most comprehensive collection of genealogical source material to be found in Britain and maybe even in the world. In England, the equivalent information is dispersed throughout St Catherine's House, London, the Public Records Office, hundreds of parish churches and scores of local libraries, archives and repositories. Here, under that elegant neo-Georgian dome, the person in search of his Scottish roots can tuck into the records of every birth, marriage and death in Scotland since 1st January 1855, into the census lists of every person living in Scotland on the relevant day in 1841, 1851, 1861, 1871, 1881 and 1891, and into 4000 volumes of old pre-1855 records from more than 900 parishes.

Clearly this treasure-house is at the heart of any research you are likely to do—and it takes up a correspondingly large part of this book, because it is difficult to conceive of any ancestor-hunter who will not rely heavily—indeed in some cases even exclusively—on the material housed in New Register House.

How do you get started at New Register House?

The first step is to "sign on," paying a specific fee to be allowed to inspect the records. The fees range from £4·50 for a day among the indexes to the post-1855 registers or £3·00 for the same period with the old parish registers or census returns to £78·50 which will allow you access to all three categories for three months. The latest charges are given in Appendix I.

Where you go after signing on will depend on which of the three collections of records you are to tackle. I shall deal with each in turn, in a logical sequence. In practice, you will of course be able to shuttle from one to another as information emerges.

There are other groups of records kept at New Register House (in addition to the well-stocked library shelves) which are listed in Appendix V.

Working at the Indexes

Births, Marriages and Deaths

How to find your great-great-great-great grandfather in a couple of hours

From 1st January 1855, every birth, marriage and death which took place in Scotland had to be registered with the civil authorities. It was one small step in the new role of central and local government which came with the industrialisation of Britain. New Register House is the home for the massive amount of paperwork produced by this single decision, 125 years' worth of Births, Marriages and Deaths at your disposal!

Scotland had, by the standards of her neighbours, been surprisingly slow to introduce statutory civil registration—England and Wales had brought it in eighteen years earlier in 1837. Scottish ancestor-hunters have tutted ever since at this delay, especially unforgiveable in a nation that had always prided itself on a sense of ancestry and the past. One compensation is that when the Scots did get around to civil registration, they did it with a thoroughness that has been the envy of those neighbours who made an earlier start.

In 1855, the exuberance was a little too uncontrolled and the certificates for that year contain an unequalled wealth of detail, which alas proved so difficult to maintain that all three categories (births, marriages and deaths) were required to make less detailed returns from 1856 onwards. Even so, the material in Scotland without exception is much more genealogically useful than its equivalent south of the Border. The death certificate provides a simple illustration of this. The death certificate in England and Wales is of value only in providing an estimated age, an address and, as a matter of interest, the cause of death. The Scottish death certificate has the advantage of indicating whether or not the person was married and if so to whom, and even more significantly of naming the parents of the dead person—an essential pointer to an earlier generation missing in the London counterpart.

Before going on to look at the statutory records, I must re-emphasise the importance of collecting, at Base One, as many copies as possible of birth, marriage and death certificates held in the family. This will help you identify additional records here at New Register House—and reduce the number of documents you have to search for there.

THE INDEXES

The first point of contact with the records of civil registration is the collection of indexes, impossible to miss when you enter the public area beneath the fine dome, nearly 1000 volumes taking up 60 yards or so of shelf space, some of them weighing quite a bit, as you will learn after a few hours searching the indexes. Genealogy can not only be fun—it can be slimming!

The indexes span all the years since 1855 and, not surprisingly, take in quite a number of technologies. You will find earlier indexes hand-written, later ones set in type and the latest ones the result of computer print-out. These different techniques for producing indexes result in the very varied size and coverage of the volumes.

The indexes are arranged in three basic groups: Births (red coding on the spine and/or cover), Marriages (green) and Deaths (black, what else?). The basic division within each group is by *year*, clearly indicated on the spine. Within each year, entries are divided into Male and Female. In earlier records, these Male and Female lists are in separate volumes (and with the hand-written indexes even further subdivided into, for example, 1855, Males A-D). The volumes are very clearly indicated but you have to keep an eye on the Male and Female volumes just in case you think you have done 1873 Males and in fact have done Females by mistake.

A special point to bear in mind when consulting these

SURNAME.	NAME. 119	PARISH OR DISTRICT	No. of Entry
Kirk	John	Culross (L.)	1
——	John	Perth (B.)	167
——	John	Hutchesontown (Glasgow)	300
——	John	Dysart (B.)	116
——	John-Samuel	High Ch. (Glasgow)	1277
——	Michael	Carnock	136
——	Ralph-Wardlaw	High Ch. (Glasgow)	495
——	Robert	Bathgate	41
——	Robert	Castle & Portsburgh (Edin.)	207
——	Robert-Hope	Kinglassie	29
——	Samuel	Penpont	28
——	Thomas	Applegarth	20
——	Thomas	Kirkmahoe	40
——	Thomas	New Monkland (L.)	69
——	Thomas-McKenzie	Kerrick	8

MIT MALE MARRIAGES—SCOTLAND—1878. MOR

Name	District	No.
MITCHELL, James	Forteviot	2
—— James Cairncross	St Andrew Edinburgh	305
—— James Chalmers	Kelvin Glasgow	569
—— James Dunlop	Kinning Park Glasgow	212
—— James G.	Tullynessle, etc.	7
—— James G.	St Peter Dundee	135
—— James Wishart	Calton Glasgow	92
—— James Y.	Blackford	10
—— John	Ladhope	2
—— John	Haggs	3
—— John	Moffat	7
—— John	Dunfermline	109
—— John	Slamannan	4
—— John	Newburgh	4
—— John	Markinch	24
—— John	Dennistoun Glasgow	114
—— John	Johnstone Renfrew	99
—— John	Kelvin Glasgow	543
—— John	Wemyss	12
—— John	Falkirk L	70
—— John	St Mary Dundee	112
—— John	Old Ardrossan	9
—— John	St Andrew Edinburgh	87
—— John	Avondale	23
—— John	Monquhitter	12
—— John	Boharm	7
—— John	Drainie	26
—— Joseph	New Deer	18
—— Joseph	St Andrew Edinburgh	52
—— Malcolm	Old Kilpatrick	13
—— Michael	Portobello	29
—— Nicol	Partick	29
—— Owen Reynolds	Old Machar Aberdeen	77
—— Patrick	Old Machar Aberdeen	309
MOIR, James	Midmar	1
—— James	Bo'ness	24
—— James	St Mary Dundee	97
—— John	Montrose	54
—— John	Maryhill	92
—— John	Monquhitter	14
—— John	Larbert	16
—— John Sinclair	Newington Edinburgh	334
—— John Wilson	St Andrews, etc. Fife	21
—— Robert	Kinning Park Glasgow	227
—— Robert	South Leith	119
—— Thomas	Montrose	20
—— Thomas Andrews	Old Machar Aberdeen	320
—— Thomas Denholm	South Leith	312
—— William	Montrose	72
—— William	South Leith	120
—— William	Larbert	22
—— William	Hutchesontown Glasgow	66
MOLLISON, Alexander	Kelso	9
—— David	Leslie Fife	6
—— Francis	Hutchesontown Glasgow	61
—— James	South Leith	188
MOLLOY, James	Calton Glasgow	262
—— Michael	Paisley	35
—— Patrick	Hutchesontown Glasgow	135
MONAGHAN, Daniel	St Andrew Dundee	28
—— Ewen	Bridgeton Glasgow	230
—— George	Abbey Paisley L	8
—— James	Paisley	235
—— John	Hutchesontown Glasgow	271
—— John	Rutherglen	66
—— Michael	Bridgeton Glasgow	313
—— Michael	Stirling	113
—— Owen	St Rollox Glasgow	[illegible]
MORE, John	Airdrie	50
—— Laurence M'Donald	Stirling	131
—— Richard	Canongate Edinburgh	237
—— Robert	St Clement Dundee	159
—— William	Lasswade	10
—— William	Newington Edinburgh	28
—— William	Blythswood Glasgow	198
MORELAND, John	Borgue	1
—— Peter	Strachur	1
MORGAN, Alexander M.	Kirkwall, etc.	28
—— Arthur	Ellon	14
—— Arthur	Boddam	13
—— David	Kelvin Glasgow	279
—— Donald	Halkirk	5
—— Donald Campbell	Kildrummy	2
—— George	Bervie	3
—— Henry	Blythswood Glasgow	120
—— Hugh	Kilbirnie	4
—— James	Dunfermline	77
—— James	Little Dunkeld	4
—— James	Alford	4
—— John	Canongate Edinburgh	12
—— John	Mid District Old Monkland	76
—— John	Blythswood Glasgow	259
—— Joseph	Holytown	11
—— Richard	Melrose	11
—— Robert	Rutherglen	90
—— Thomas	South Leith	66
—— Thomas	Mid District Old Monkland	105
—— William	Partick	119
—— Wilson	Airdrie	182
M[illegible], Alexander	Barvas	2
—— Archibald	Kilmarnock	58

MCC

NAME.	AGE.	REGISTRATION DISTRICT. NAME.	NO.	ENTRY NO.
MCCONNELL				
DAVID	84	BELLSHILL	625	11
DONALD SWAN	16	GLASGOW	645.3	439
DONALD SWAN	62	OLD KILPATRICK	501	251
IAN	0	IRVINE	595	387
IAN CALLANDAR	52	AIRDRIE	651	45
JACOB	82	STONEHAVEN	255	26
JAMES	84	CARLUKE	629	111
JAMES	92	GLASGOW	644.5	414
JAMES	74	GLASGOW	644.3	601
JAMES	60	JOHNSTONE RENFREW	565	188
JOHN	66	ARMADALE	662.2	9
JOHN	66	AYR	578	344
JOHN	59	MOTHERWELL ETC	628	519

indexes is that they refer to the year in which the event was registered and not the year in which it happened. In most cases, the two will be the same, but occasionally you will find an event appearing in the indexes the year after it took place. This is not only in obvious cases where end-of-the-year hatches, matches and despatches hang over from the December to the January, but also in a small number of cases when, after the normal period allowed for registration, evidence comes to light of, say, a birth which has not been registered. Defaulting parents would be reminded of their obligation and the entry duly made—and indexed for the point at which the information is registered.

An aside: at some stage earlier or later you will probably come across problems of naming arising from illegitimacy. Appendix IV outlines some of the factors to bear in mind in these instances.

1. Births

Births offer the simplest of the indexes—you have no real choice. If you are looking up the birth of James Smith or Jane Smith, that is that: you have no alternative. When you have found the one you are looking for, note the registration district and the entry number. These, along with the year, are enough to identify precisely any birth registration.

You should realise that in the case of Births, Marriages and Deaths, unless you are absolutely sure that the entry you have tracked down is the right one (an unusual name, a precise date or a small registration district would help here), you should note down *all* possible entries to fall back on in case your first leads you to a dead end. When you eventually get up to see the register and find that it's not your William Robertson, it is a good idea to have another likely individual at hand to follow up—and will save you a lot of time.

Where there is a middle name—a practice which came well into fashion over the period we are talking about—this can often prove a help to sorting out your man from a host of contenders. You should not however assume that the absence of a middle name for which you are looking means that the person is not the right one. Often the name was added later in life and may appear on marriage or death certificates but not on birth certificates. Conversely, a name given at birth may disappear by the time a person marries or dies.

2. Marriages

Here the format is very similar, but now of course you are actually looking for *two* people, so you have a choice of which one to go for. (In fact, as the woman is listed by both maiden and married name, you have a choice of three). The choice enables you to avoid some of the problems associated with having a common name or combination of names to look up. Let us say you are looking for a marriage between William Robertson and Jane Alexander. All the names are fairly common in Scotland, so you would probably go for the Jane Alexander combination which will be a little bit easier. When you find a likely Jane Alexander entry, you can check that there is a corresponding Jane Robertson or William Robertson entry to match. This will confirm beyond reasonable doubt that you have the right pair.

Be on the look-out for any way in which you can simplify your search. A particular warning is needed for the Mac names. In the indexes "Mac" appears in a different spot from "Mc" (unlike the modern telephone directories which treat forms of the prefix as the same). If there was a clear distinction between the two forms, there would be no problem other than that of human error, but the modern concept of "correct" spelling was certainly not widespread in the nineteenth century. Not only might the clerk who is filling in the form spell it differently from your forebear—that forebear himself might not have any standard way of doing it. In most cases, there was a cheerfully haphazard attitude to spelling—I have instances of an Alexander Macfarlane who *signed* his name with three different spellings in the four examples of his signature which I have found! The upshot of this type of inconsistency is that to be sure of checking a Mac name you have to look up "Mac" and "Mc" separately in each volume. That is very time-consuming, so if possible in marriages avoid the Mac partner, except for confirming an entry.

It is not only the surnames that can help—double Christian names or unusual Christian names can also help you track down someone with a common surname.

As in the case of Births, the correct entry in the index will give you a unique identification combination for a Marriage—year, registration district, entry number. This is all you need to locate the exact entry.

3. Deaths

Once again, the female entries are listed twice: once under maiden name and once, when the woman was married, under her married name. This again reflects the Scottish recognition of the importance of a woman's independent name—and explains the excessively heavy Female indexes in Marriages and Deaths!

This gives you an option if you are looking up a female death. It will be much easier to find Ann Girdwood Miller under Ann Girdwood than Ann Miller.

An even more useful innovation—relating to both males and females, married and single—came in 1868 when the death indexes included the age of the person involved. You will probably find for yourself the frustration of looking up lots of William Robertsons in the early death indexes only to find they are infants and certainly not the aged patriarch you are seeking. After 1868, the entry "Robertson, William, 5" will tell you that he is not for you and the entry "Robertson, William, 73" will raise your hopes. But remember these ages are often inaccurate, so don't rule out that 73-year-old Willie just because you know the one you are looking for would have been 76 in that year.

I have indicated the ways which are available to you to try and minimise the chores of hunting for people with common names. It is worth at this stage mentioning the other side of the coin—dealing with a family with an unusual name. If the name is a rare one, it may be worth your while making a note of *all* references to it in the indexes even if you do not at this stage intend to look at those registrations. In this way, you can identify previously unknown branches, or see certain patterns of names and geographical locations. When, for example, I was searching for members of my wife's family—Balbirnie—it was easy to identify a large clump of Tayside names, a smaller one in the West of Scotland and another in Edinburgh. The Christian name distribution was distinctive: Peter and David only appeared in Tayside, Charles and Henry only in the West, Robert and Alexander only in Edinburgh. When I came across a Robert, out of place in Glasgow, I followed it up—and found he had moved through from Edinburgh and was indeed one of ours.

This "total" logging of index entries can only be justified when the name is truly unusual—and the indexes themselves will tell you whether or not that is the case.

FROM INDEXES TO ENTRIES

Having tracked down the relative you are seeking, you have enough information to identify the exact entry in the civil registers. In theory, in order to find out what information is carried, you have to order a copy of that entry from the Registrar-General, a procedure which can take a few days or perhaps even a week or so. There is naturally a charge made for this service, the current tariff being shown in Appendix I. The copy incidentally may take the form of either a direct photostat of the entry or the details typed on to a *pro forma* sheet.

This service is open to all, with the alternative of being able to collect the copies or have them posted to you. It is quite expensive and, for genealogical purposes, a little slow, delaying the time at which you can make use of the information on the records to move forward to the next stage.

This is where the more common alternative comes on to the scene. The Registrar-General has for many years—and it is worth stressing, as James VI and I used to do to his Parliament, the privilege comes by grace and not by right—allowed people to inspect the actual entries and take notes without addition to the original fee charged for inspecting the indexes. This privilege is perhaps the most important single difference between England and Scotland as far as the genealogist is concerned. It cuts down the cost and time involved in building up a pedigree (family tree or chart), as well as allowing you to see the signature or cross of a forebear and come to some assessment of how literate he may have been!

In order to be fair to all those wanting to make use of this privilege—and to minimise queues—access to the registers is limited to half-an-hour or six entries.

How do you get to see the record of, say, your grandfather's birth registration?

You have, let us assume, tracked him down in the Births indexes for 1876. You have discovered that the birth was registered in Perth, and the entry was 118. (This is a fictitious example—we'll have plenty of real ones later on).

You look up, on the wall chart, the reference number for Perth and find it is 435. You now have all of the information you need, so you put your name down on the waiting list (kept on the public counter) and wait until you are called. This can take anything from a couple of minutes (off the tourist season) to perhaps half-an-hour or more in the summer months.

The Repository Assistant will then take you to the area in which the Birth records are kept (Births on the ground floor, Marriages on the first and Deaths on the second). He will produce the relevant volume and open it at the correct entry. You may then take down the details. Small tables are provided alongside the bookshelves.

This is where all that work you did at home drawing up the sheets of your notebook comes in helpful, for you have on your page all the headings which appear in the records and all the details you should record. (Incidentally, consider the time you have taken to get in front of this open book and don't skimp on the notes. Items such as the name of the informant (the person giving the information to the registrar) may seem unimportant at the moment, but you never know when that fact may be of some value).

The procedure is exactly the same for the other records relating to Marriages and Deaths. It is a good idea to try and get as many of each together for inspection at the same time. Naturally, however, in the early stages in particular, it will not be possible to ask for three marriages or two deaths as you are really looking for the information on one key entry to get you going.

So you've reached the stage of collecting details from the Births, Marriages and Deaths entries. What will the entries tell you—and what should you especially keep an eye out for? I shall deal with each of the categories in turn, showing what information is carried—and adding, just in case you strike the jackpot, just what bonuses await you if you land on one of those 1855 entries which carried so much extra material.

THE BIRTH CERTIFICATE

1. Check

First of all check the name of the person and any other detail you know which will confirm that you are in fact looking at the right entry. When you are sure this is really your man (or woman), make a note of the details as they appear.

2. Amendments

Pay particular attention to the first narrow column which is so easily overlooked and is rarely, if ever, mentioned in the books on genealogy. This shows whether or not an addition

1863. BIRTHS in the District of Canongate in the Burgh of Edinburgh

	No.	Name and Surname. (1.)	When and Where Born. (2.)	Sex. (3.)	Name, Surname, & Rank or Profession of Father. Name, and Maiden Surname of Mother. Date and Place of Marriage. (4.)	Signature and Qualification of Informant, and Residence, if out of the House in which the Birth occurred. (5.)	When and Where Registered, and Signature of Registrar. (6.)
	529	Robert Thomson	1863 May First 9h 30m P.M. Dumbiedykes Place Edinburgh	M	John Thomson Clerk. Brewery Jane Thomson M.S. Mulholland 1862 June 20th Edinburgh	John Thomson Father	1863 May 22nd at Edinburgh Thomas Hardie Assistant Registrar AB R
	530	Thomas Muir	1863 May Second 2h A.M. 49 High Street Edinburgh	M	George Muir Bookbinder Journeyman Margaret Muir M.S. Clark 1845 December 2nd Leith	Margaret Muir Mother	1863 May 22nd at Edinburgh Thomas Hardie Assistant Registrar AB R
	531	Janet Catherine Hay Balbirnie	1863 May Second 10h A.M. 17 Arthur Street Edinburgh	F	James Dundas Balbirnie Clerk Publishers Isabella Balbirnie M.S. McFarlane 1846 June 3rd Edinburgh	Jas. D. Balbirnie Father	1863 May 22nd at Edinburgh Thomas Hardie Assistant Registrar AB R

or amendment to the entry exists and if so gives you a reference number. Once an entry is made it cannot be altered—but it can be augmented. In the case of a birth certificate, for example, an additional name or a paternity action may be recorded elsewhere. If this is the case, that little first column will tell you. It doesn't crop up very often, but when it does it can provide valuable information. Ask the Repository Assistant to help you find the supplementary entry which is kept in a different section of the bookshelves.

3. The names

The name of the person: take down all the names—they may come in useful in establishing name patterns and relatives.

4. The address

Where and when born: unlike the English certificates, the time of birth is given in all cases (south of the Border a distinction reserved for twins and other multiple births)—perhaps the only element of no genealogical significance. Astrologers may find the fact of interest. Note the address, as you may need it for Census leads.

5. Sex

You will already know this from the Index and the name, so again it can be left out of your notes.

6. Parents' details

Note name and profession of father: there may be a variation from any facts you already know; name and maiden name of mother (very important); the date and place of their wedding—a really significant item (yet another example of the value of Scottish records as opposed to those elsewhere in Britain). One point worth making: don't be too surprised if the date turns out to be slightly inaccurate—this was before the widespread celebration of wedding anniversaries and many a spouse was less than precise when it came to this fact.

1890. MARRIAGES in the DISTRICT of SOUTH LEITH in the COUNTY of EDINBURGH

No.	When, Where, and How Married.	Signatures of Parties. Rank or Profession, Whether Single or Widowed, and Relationship (if any).	Age.	Usual Residence.	Name, Surname, and Rank or Profession of Father. Name, and Maiden Surname of Mother.	If a regular Marriage, Signatures of officiating Minister and Witnesses. If irregular, Date of Conviction, Decree of Declarator, or Sheriff's Warrant.	When & Where Registered, and Signature of Registrar.
117	1890. on the Twenty fourth day of April at 7 Kirk Street Leith	(Signed) Hugh Cleland, Bookbinder [illegible] Master, Bachelor	30	3 [illegible] Edinr	Wm Cleland, [illegible]; Grace Cleland m.s. Blackhall	(Signed) J. S. [illegible] Minister	1890. April 25 At Leith
	After Banns according to the forms of the U.P. Church	(Signed) Isabella C. Crighton, Spinster	28	7 Kirk Street Leith	Gavin Crighton, Marine engineer; Susanna Crighton m.s. Cochrane	(Signed) David Cleland, Witness; Annie Crighton, Witness	[illegible] Registrar.
118	1890. on the Twenty fifth day of April at 1 [illegible] Place Leith	(Signed) T. Bryden, Carter, Bachelor	21	13 Gordon Street Leith	William Bryden, Carter; Janet Bryden m.s. McQueen	(Signed) D. Cockburn, minister of [illegible] Leith Church	1890. April 26 At Leith
	After Banns according to the forms of the Free Church	(Signed) Maggie Stewart, Spinster	17	21 Ferrier Street Leith	Thomas Stewart, Boilermaker (deceased); Janet Stewart m.s. Harris (deceased)	(Signed) James Goodie, Witness; [illegible] Stewart, Witness	[illegible] Registrar.
	(1.)	(2.)	(3.)	(4.)	(5.)	(6.)	(7.)

I have come across one Scot who gave a different date on the certificates of his four children—and not one of them agreed with the date in the parish records! This important detail—the date and place of the parents' marriage—was omitted from the certificates from 1856 to 1860, inclusive of both years. If your ancestor was born in this "blank" period it is worth checking up on his brothers and sisters to get the information, as it will most likely refer to the pre-1855 period when you will need to know parish and date to stand any chance of success.

7. Signature of informant

This also gives qualification/relationship and address if different from the one at which the birth took place: information which could be of value—make a note of it.

As you see, the typical birth certificate (there will be minor changes from one period to another) carries a wealth of information. Not the least of this is the fact that it is the only certificate where the age of the person concerned (zero) can be guaranteed with any precision!

The 1855 Bonus stated, in addition, whether or not the birth took place in lodgings, the parents' ages and birthplaces, and other issue both living and deceased!

THE MARRIAGE CERTIFICATE

With two people involved, the marriage certificate is naturally the most heavily congested of the three as far as information is concerned. It is therefore especially important that you do not miss details in the general *embarras de richesse.*

1. Amendment

There is again a space to note any addition or amendment. I have not yet come across such an item but keep an eye out and ask your co-operative Repository Assistant if anything appears there. A reference there could refer not only to a clerical error but also to a divorce or, rarely, to a bigamous marriage.

2. The wedding ceremony

Details include date, place (sometimes a church, sometimes the house of the bride—in any case make a note as it may come in handy later on) whether, in the case of marriages before 1st January 1978, performed after Banns or by licence, the Church according to whose forms it was performed. (Note: this may provide a useful guide to the Church the family belonged to—a valuable point when it comes to the pre-1855 searches). You will also come across the "irregular" marriages including the well-known "Gretna Green" type. You will find a note on these in Appendix III.

3. The groom

Details of name, occupation, condition (bachelor, widower), age (a useful guide but never to be taken as gospel), address (handy for tracking down his family in census returns), name and occupation of father, name and maiden name of mother. Take down all details, even when you think you have them from other sources—a man's description of his job, for example, may change slightly but significantly.

4. The bride

Similar details to those given for the groom, although it is not common to give occupation. As in the case of the man, the listing of the parents usually indicated when one or both of these is dead at the time of the marriage. Generally speaking, if a parent is listed as "deceased" this can be taken as proof: in the mere absence of the word "deceased" you should not accept for certain that this is the case. This is a not unknown oversight of omission.

5. The witnesses

Do not neglect to record who signed the certificate. The names usually include the minister officiating (he can always be checked from directories if there seems to be some relationship indicated by the name), the best man/relative of the groom, and the bridesmaid/relative of the bride. Note them—they may be of some use.

6. Registrar

There is rarely any point in making a note of this item.

The 1855 Bonus is, in the case of the Marriage certificates, less spectacular and more restricted than in the Birth and Death certificates. In that year, there was a distinction made between present and usual residence and both were stated and, in addition, details were given of any former marriages and the number of children, living and deceased, from these.

THE DEATH CERTIFICATE

As I hinted earlier, thc Scottish certificate differs dramatically in its value to ancestor-seekers in comparison with the English record, which rarely provides more than the barest gravestone. Look out for the following:

1. That little first column

This will tell you if there was a Fatal Accident Enquiry and will even lead you to the findings of that enquiry. In the case of the death on 24 September 1884 of a seven-year-old girl, Margaret Mackay, I noticed the reference in the first column and discovered from Corrections 685/2 Vol VI, Page 2, that the head injuries referred to in the Death Certificate had been caused when the child, playing in one of those towering Edinburgh tenements while waiting for her tea, fell from the banisters and was killed. In some cases an incident such as this might lead you to a newspaper report.

455	Leitch Robert Laborer	Male	74 years	Kirkalday Fife 50 years	John Leitch Miner Sophia Leitch maiden name Penman	Catherine Leitch maiden name Anderson	1 Robert Dead 2 Helen 47 years 3 Mary 43 do 4 Andrew 42 do 5 James dead 6 Jessie do 7 Thomas do
456	Lyall Robert Brewer	Male	46 years	Dunbar 18 years	Robert Lyall Trade or Profession unknown Mother's name unknown	Ann Lyall maiden name Chisholm	No issue

1855 September 27 at 11 hours 35 minutes P.M.	Water of Leith Edinburgh	Paralysis which continued for 8 years not certified no medical man called	West Church Burying Ground as certified by Alexr Russell Undertaker	Adam Leitch Son	1855 September 28th at 14 Lothian Road Edinburgh J Thomson Registrar
1855 September 26th at 5 hours 30 minutes P.M.	Sunbury Distillery Edinburgh	Killed by a fall no surgeon called	Old Greyfriars Burying Ground as certified by John Paxton undertaker	Robert Dodds Stepson	1855 September 29th at 14 Lothian Road Edinburgh J Thomson Registrar

2. Name and details of person

Again note the profession which is given and also details of any marriages. In the case of a married woman dying, the occupation of her husband is given.

3. Where did the death occur?

Here you are told not only the place of the actual death, but also the home address of the person concerned where this is different. In the case of death in hospital, for example, this is a valuable addition.

4. How old was the person?

Make a note of it, even although it may not be absolutely accurate.

5. Parents

The names of both parents are given, together with profession of father and maiden name of mother.

6. Cause of death

Even if the medical terms seem complex and irrelevant, try and get them down. The column will also tell you how long the disease had persisted and the name of the medical attendant.

7. The informant

Do not neglect this column which tells you who gave the information to the Registrar, in what capacity (usually a stated relationship to the deceased or, for example, landlord or neighbour where the person was living in rented property). These details are important for two distinct reasons. Firstly, they may help you establish other family relationships: when for example I saw from the death certificate of one James T. B. Alexander that the informant was a brother-in-law, Mr Ralph Linton, it told me that the deceased had a sister who had at one stage married Mr Linton. Secondly, by knowing who had furnished the information, you are more able to assess whether or not it is likely to be reliable in the difficult details. Despite the example of the certificate for the famous Scots Socialist, Keir Hardie, where his half-brother was clearly not aware of the fact that they were not full brothers, a person's brother can usually be trusted to provide the names of the parents with some precision; the keeper of a boarding house will be less reliable.

The 1855 Bonus can, in the case of the Death Certificate, be enormous, spanning an incredible period of years. It gave in addition to the already full standard death certificate mentioned above: place of birth, details of marriages, burial place (a useful tip-off if there are tombstones still in existence) and a list of all issue living or deceased!

A specific example will give you some idea of just what is possible if you hit on the right person dying in 1855:

> William Balbirnie, a copper engraver specialising in music printing, died 9th May 1855. We are told that he lived at 391 Lawnmarket, that he died of consumption and had been troubled by it for two years, that he was 56 years old (an accurate detail as it turns out—his 57th birthday would have come nine days later), that he had seven children (with names), that he had been married to Catherine Johnstone, and that he was buried in the Old South Ground, Calton Cemetery. His parents were given as James Balbirnie, shoemaker, and Ann Dundas.

That is a considerable amount of information from a single document, accurate in nearly every detail. It included the name and occupation of a father who was born in 1760 and was provided by the deceased's son, who was to die in 1871—a span of 111 years as far as personalities are concerned.

The information in this case was precise: it was provided by a son who was a commercial clerk, used presumably to precise data and able to give details of his grandparents as they had in fact both died at advanced ages (80) so that he must have known them well. The only detail he slipped up on in fact was when, listing the children (his brothers and sisters), he had to include a sister who had died as a baby when he was only two years old. She had been christened Bethea—he listed her as Bythnia—a vessel of that name was at that time involved in the Crimea activities and may have influenced his version!

This indicates the problem at the root of the high ambitions held by those who framed the first Scottish registrations. The ability to provide all those facts and figures depended so much on the informant. In our example, the man was not dying at an advanced age. Suppose he had been 80? Would anyone be able to provide the sort of information being asked? And if there were no relatives around, an old man dying in a hospital or lodgings would invariably mean a certificate with more blanks than completed columns. These were probably the reasons behind the discontinuing of the detailed records in 1856—and might even mean that you could hit the jackpot (1855) and still be disappointed with a number of unanswered questions when you come to see the actual entry.

That completes a rundown of what you can expect to find in the post-1855 records of Births, Marriages and Deaths. I shall outline in a similar manner what is contained in the other two great treasuries of information held by the Registrar-General—the Censuses and the Old Parish Records (pre-1855)—and then show, with actual case-histories, just how these three can be combined to produce a fine scaffolding of family relationships on which to build your family history.

The Census Returns 1841-1891

Where was your great-great-granny on the evening of 31 March 1851?

In 1801, Britain made its first attempt to count the heads in the kingdom—and did it again in 1811, 1821 and 1831. These were of little value to the genealogist as we have, except in some rare cases, only the actual totals with no details of individuals. On 7 June 1841, however, the first door-to-door, person-to-person census was carried out in Britain, for which we have the detailed enumerators' transcript books. These, carrying the name, occupation and approximate age of 2,620,184 people living in Scotland on that day, make up the second great source of raw material for the Scot in search of his roots. As with civil registration, the census has led many a researcher to sigh and ask why it had not been started much earlier.

The answer is perhaps a simple one. In the stable, even static society which characterised pre-industrial Britain, there was no obvious need for a census—and certainly not for a census which itemised individuals. There had been an attempt, as early as 1753, to instigate a national (i.e. British) census, but Parliament had rejected the proposals. A deciding factor in the rebuttal was the stance of the religious objectors. They found a clear warning at the end of Samuel's lengthy contribution to the Old Testament when "David, tempted by Satan, forceth Joab to number the people" and, one might add, produceth some rather nasty manifestations of the Lord's anger. Not even that same Lord's apparent pleasure at a later tax-oriented census, making it the occasion for the birth of Christ, could make up for Samuel's clear warning that censuses were evil.

Nevertheless, the transformation of Britain brought about by the arrival of the machine and the factory saw a flight from the countryside to the towns, and the authorities decided that some attempts should be made to chart these changes. The Ordnance Survey was set up before the end of the eighteenth century as one way of doing this. The civil registration which we have looked at in the preceding section was another. In between these two came Britain's first Census—in 1801. This, a strictly statistical exercise in which households were numbered but not named, was the first of a series of regular ten-yearly censuses which have been held right up to the present census year of 1981—with the sole exception of 1941 when Britons had other things to worry about.

It is worth emphasising at this point the particularly valuable contribution that the census returns since 1841 make to genealogical research in Scotland. While the census was a *British* affair (as opposed to civil registration which was undertaken by the Scots, English, Welsh and Irish in different ways and at different times), it had an extra significance in Scotland.

Firstly, because Scottish civil registration did not take place until 1855, the census returns contain information about people *not covered by the statutory records.* This is in distinct contrast to the state of affairs in England and Wales where the first useful census (1841) took place four years *after* total registration of births, marriages and deaths was introduced, so that individuals were already being caught in the main records net *before* the census was set up. In Scotland on the other hand civil registration as we have seen came into effect four years *after* the second (1851) census. Clearly the returns of 1841 and 1851 will carry names and details of very many people not covered by the post-1855 records.

Secondly, there is also a Scottish bonus in the later census returns. As the information given at censuses is confidential, it is not released to the public until a century has elapsed. This rule would give searchers access to the returns for 1841, 1851, 1861 and 1871. In Scotland, however, there is a more liberal attitude to this confidentiality aspect and researchers are allowed to see and make notes from (but not publish details of) the census returns for 1881 and 1891.

These two elements give the census a much more important part in Scottish genealogical investigation than is normally suggested in books written on a broader (and that generally means English-oriented) basis.

So the enormous fund of information represented by the census returns is at your disposal. Where is it? How do you "plug in"? What will you find when you get hold of the material? The answers to those questions come rather in the form of a Good News/Bad News/Good News story.

Good news

Once again the returns are stored in the same building as the statutory records—New Register House at the East End of Princes Street, Edinburgh. And once again, access is a simple matter, as I shall explain later.

Bad news

There is no indexing of the census returns other than by town or village or, in the case of the cities, by street. That means that you have to know, not the personal details of an individual (which were enough to lead you to the exact entry in the statutory records), but where he was living on the day that the census was taken. But don't be too perturbed—it is usually possible to answer, with some degree of accuracy, such questions as "Where was your great-great granny on the evening of 31 March 1855?"

Good news

When you do find the right entries you will be rewarded with a variety of details which can either tell you something fresh about your ancestors or, no less important, identify new people to follow up in the statutory records or the earlier Old Parochial Records.

Back to the procedures. As before, you need to pay a search fee which will allow you to look at the census returns. This can be taken out for a day, a week, a month or a quarter and the costs are shown in Appendix I of this book. It is worth emphasising that this time your search will be carried out in a different part of the building and, as a leaflet from the Registrar-General puts it, "accommodation in the Search Room is limited and admission cannot be guaranteed." In essence that means: try and check in advance that there is room for you; and avoid May-September when there is a pressure on space. Better still, book in advance—a facility especially useful to out-of-town (or even out-of-Scotland) visitors.

Having paid up and signed on, you will be allocated a desk in the Search Room and the indexes are waiting for you. I mentioned that the censuses were not indexed by individual—and this bit of bad news has at least one consolation: instead of the 60 yards of indexes staring at you for the civil records you now have less than a metre of bookshelf to worry about!

Your work on the Births, Marriages and Deaths records will have given you a number of events which provide addresses to try in the census returns. Obviously the nearer these events are to an actual census date, the better chance you stand of finding your ancestors in! In the case of city dwellers, the trade directories can sometimes provide an alternative means of finding an address near a census date—but bear in mind that such directories are usually prepared the year before the date shown on the cover. Let's take an example:

> Having from a street directory discovered that Hugh Dalrymple Alexander M.D. had his surgery at 46 Canongate and lived at 21 St John Street, Edinburgh, we look up St John Street in the Edinburgh 1851 Census Street Index. (If it had been a rural address, we would look up the parish in the General 1851 Census index). We find that the street is in Census District 685-3 and is covered in enumerators' books 75 and 76.

We fill in our requisition slip for CEN 51, 685-3, 75/6. We get bound manuscript books containing numbers 75 and 76 (these numbers are given in the blue covers) and we work our way through the pages looking at the address column for St John Street. When we find it, we look for number 21—the numbers, especially of main roads, are not always in sequence as they follow the sequence in which the enumerator visited the houses and that may have involved leaving the road and covering alleys or sidestreets. This time, we have a short and straightforward street and soon find the entry. It reads as follows:

CENSUS 1851

21 St John Street, Edinburgh

1. Hugh D Alexander
   Head of household, married, age 33, Physician, Surgeon M.D. St Andrews, Glasgow, General Practitioner, born Dumfries.
2. Jessie Alexander, age 32, wife, born Midlothian, Edinburgh.
3. Mary Alexander, daughter, age 7, born Midlothian, Edinburgh.
4. William Alexander, son, age 6, born Midlothian, Edinburgh.
5. Jessie Alexander, daughter, age 5, born Midlothian, Edinburgh.
6. Agnes Alexander, daughter, age 3, born Midlothian, Edinburgh.
7. Hugh Alexander, son, age 2, born Midlothian, Edinburgh.
8. John Alexander, son, age 6 months, born Midlothian, Edinburgh.
9. Denham S. Kerr Alexander, brother, age 21, 4th year Medical student, born Dumfries.
10. Margaret King, servant, unmarried, age 19, born Ireland.
11. Mary Lee, domestic servant, unmarried, age 19, born Edinburgh.

This gives us a very wide variety of genealogical information (notably the birthplace of Dr Alexander, the names and approximate birth dates of his wife, three daughters and three sons) and family information (he was a physician and surgeon and had obtained his degree in St Andrews). In addition we get the bonus fact that his brother, Denham S. Kerr Alexander, is following in his footsteps, but this time at the University of Edinburgh. The existence of two servants tells us something of the family's social standing.

From the genealogical point of view, the great value of this type of information is that it takes us well back beyond the 1855 frontier with clear pointers that we are, for example, to look for Dr Alexander's birth certificate in one of the Dumfries parishes in the year 1817 or 1818.

This simple, but real, example shows just how the census returns can be used to build up a network of people. There is naturally an element of luck involved. In that example, we found what turned out to be the entire family still living with their parents. Ten years later, some may have flown the nest.

Another aspect of the luck element is that it is not always possible to find the people you are looking for at home on the night of a census. While this would be more likely to apply to say a sailor than a lawyer, a commercial traveller than a grocer, it is worth remembering that, at the time we are talking about, travel was still a slow business and visits to relatives or business trips of what we would today consider to be short distances could, in those days, take people away from home for lengthy periods. I have had several examples of bad luck of this sort, but had it all repaid when I had one stroke of good luck. A census was held on the day of a particular person's funeral—and that enabled me to discover, staying the night, a knot of country cousins I would never otherwise have traced! The other side of that coin was that anyone looking for those country cousins at their end would have found an empty house.

shewing how Entries may be made.

1			2			3	4	
PLACE	HOUSES		NAME and SURNAME, SEX, and AGE, of each Person who abode in each House on the Night of 6th June.			OCCUPATION	WHERE BORN	
Here insert Name of Village, Street, Square, Close, Court, &c.	Uninhabited or Building	Inhabited	NAME and SURNAME	AGE Male	AGE Female	Of what Profession, Trade, Employment, or whether of Independent Means.	If Born in Scotland, state whether in County or otherwise.	Whether Foreigner, or whether Born in England or Ireland.
George Street		1	James Johnson	40		Chemist	Y.	
			Jane do.		35		N.	
			William do.	15		Shoem. Ap.	Y.	
			Anne do.		13		Y.	
			Edward Wallace	30		Chemist's Sh.	N.	
			Sarah Robins		45	F. S.		I.
do.	1U	1	John Lockhart	60		Publican	N.	
do.	1B		Mary do.		45		Y.	
do.	1B		Ellen do.		20		N.	
			James Macpherson	25		M. S.		
			Henry Wilson	35		Army	N.	
			n. k.	above 20				
Chapel Row		1	William Grant	50		Farmer	Y.	
			Elizabeth do.		40		E.	
			William do.	15		Navy	Y.	
			Charlotte do.		8		Y.	
			n. k. do.		5 months		Y.	
			Richard Clerk	20		Ag. Lab.	N.	
do.	1U	1	Robert Macdowall	45		Tailor	Y.	
			Martha do.		30		Y.	
			John Muller	25		Tailor J.		F.
			Ann Maclean		20	F. S.	N.	
do.		1	Eaward Johnstone	35		Ind.	N.	
			Charles do.	30		Cl.	N.	
			James Leary	20		M. S.		I.
TOTAL in Page	2U 2B	5		15	10			

What do the censuses tell us?

Censuses were not established to help people build up a family tree or write a family history. They were set up by central government to provide it with certain information which it felt it needed to have. That information changed as circumstances changed and today we have a much more comprehensive and sophisticated census, with selected samples providing more detailed information than could ever have been imagined by the 1841 authorities. In each census, what you are in fact going to be looking at are the enumerators' transcripts from their original forms on to printed books. The legibility of the writing and the permanence of the ink vary considerably and the feature of checking through a long street is the way in which these change. With one book you are delighted with a bold black script—at the next you are struggling with a spidery sepia hand. The material is rarely if ever totally incomprehensible—and the staff will lend a friendly hand if you are really stuck.

The 1841 Census took place on 7 June 1841 and its main importance lies in the fact that it provides early information some fourteen years before Scotland's civil registration. The enumerators were given forms to fill in, and, as you see from the sample printed for their guidance, their returns were to give the following information:

a. the address of the dwelling house
b. the name of the individual
c. the age of the individual (rounded down to the nearest 5)
d. the status, profession or occupation
e. the answer to the question "whether born in the country or not"
f. whether or not the individual is foreign.

The fact that the Government of the time was concerned primarily with the movement of people in this age of social upheaval is underlined by the questions relating to origin. The genealogist will bemoan the fact that he is not told the relationship of individuals to one another (although it is usually possible to guess with some degree of accuracy) or the exact age of the people (which would simplify later investigations of the Old Parochial Registers).

The 1851 Census was held on 31 March 1851 and marked a great step forward on three distinct fronts:

a. the relationship to the head of the household was indicated (together with the "condition" of the person concerned—married, unmarried, widowed)

b. the age was given accurately—although it is worth noting that the accuracy which was intended was not always achieved. Women in particular rarely seemed to age ten years between the decennial censuses—my own record is finding one who aged only three years between the 1851 and 1861 Census. The ages are naturally reasonably accurate in the lower ranges.

c. the place of birth is given in much greater detail, often down to the exact parish, which is a great help when we come to look at the Old Parochial Registers.

Each census seems to have had its own little idiosyncrasy which can, in an admittedly limited number of cases, throw extra light on the family. In the case of 1851 Census, there is a question asking whether the individual is blind or deaf-and-dumb. This perhaps represents the establishment's concern with social matters.

The 1861 Census was held on 8 April 1861 and was the first to be held after the introduction of statutory records in Scotland. This means that it deals only with those people who can be found also in the civil registrations. Its value would therefore seem to be limited to the sort of short-cut role indicated in our earlier example. It does, however, have the benefit of including a new question—indicating a further concern for social matters—namely, how many of the rooms occupied by the family contain one or more windows. It also

Census records can vary from precisely numbered streets of a city to a rather rambling walkabout in a rural parish

frequently indicates whether the person was an employer and, when he was, how many people he employed.

These details help the researcher to learn something of the living conditions and financial position of his ancestors—an aspect which would not really emerge from the Births, Marriages and Deaths records.

Subsequent censuses, held on 3 April 1871, 4 April 1881 and 5 April 1891, follow very closely the now established format and the only really different information you are likely to discover comes with the latter censuses which indicate whether or not an individual speaks Gaelic. Again this would apply in only a minority of instances but where it is applicable offers a fascinating little sidelight..

I have concentrated on the role of the census returns in combining with the statutory records and, as we shall see in the next chapter, with the Old Parochial Registers, together with the additional role of supplying those extras about disabilities, housing, Gaelic-speaking etc. There is another small way in which they can offer facts which are not given elsewhere—and that is in telling you something of what the females did. In many of the marriage records, we are not told what the bride did for a living, although the groom's occupation is nearly always supplied. The censuses, taken in the family home *before* the marriage, will often tell you just what job the girl had (if any) and sometimes in quite useful detail. Such examples as "straw-bonnet maker," "shop assistant in draper's" or "works in tobacconist shop" all surely add something to a knowledge of the person who is otherwise going to become little more than a wife-and-mother statistic.

By far the greatest value of the censuses lies, to my mind, in their ability to fit a person or a family into an environment. Whenever I am making notes about a family from the census returns, I invariably make a note of the neighbours or, in a small village, of a wider spread of the community. I want to know just what sort of people lived nearby or what families dominated the village or, in the towns, who shared the same front door.

Surely part of the story of any family is not just who they were, when they flourished and what they did. I feel that I know much more of one of my wife's ancestors when I learn that he lived in the same building as a groom, a telegraph engineer (one day I'll find out just what that meant in 1851!), a blacksmith, a newspaper office clerk, a brass founder and an animal portrait painter—and that just below him dwelt an Irish police constable and his wife, together with a mother-in-law and five working brothers-in-law!

Sometimes the census returns can give you the flavour of a period or a place in a way which cannot be matched by the history books. The returns for 25 Carrubbers Close, Edinburgh for example show that in 1841 that crowded alley, which today forms a back lane for one of the capital's most respectable department stores, housed an unbelievable congestion of trades crammed into the 41 flats that shared the stair of number 25. Amongst the many shoemakers and tailors, glaziers and jewellers, cow-feeders and boot-closers jostled a large number of FS (female servants). Their presence is perhaps explained by the final entry of a husband-and-wife declaring themselves to be "fleshers" (butchers). The supervisor of the enumerator has deleted the word "flesher" and inserted in red ink "brothel keeper."

The history books and social history studies may give you the story of the country, the contemporary newspapers may relate that to an area or a city, but only the census returns can take you down to the details of a village, a street or even a house.

Old Parochial Records

Beyond 1855—where Births, Marriages and Deaths turn into Baptisms, Banns and Burials

Leafing through the records of baptisms in the ancient Canongate records which include in their earliest marriages that of Mary, Queen of Scots and Darnley, I came to an abrupt halt. There was an entry crossed out! I could understand a marriage entry being erased at the last moment and possibly, thanks to a brisk, reviving Scottish breeze, even a burial entry, but a birth entry?

I could not avoid reading through it, rather as the jury always seems to perk up and pay attention when the judge orders a particular testimony to be "struck from the records." The baptism seemed quite normal if a little bit up market. A Scottish aristocrat and his lady, with some impressive kinsfolk as witnesses, were playing their part in recording a perhaps long-awaited heir. But the whole entry was scored out and in the margin was written:

> "His Lordship refused to pay the clerk his fee and this entry is accordingly rased out"!

That example underlines the one basic truth about the pre-1855 records: they were certainly not, nor were they intended to be, total and comprehensive. They had for many decades before 1855 meant paying out a sum of money, and the noble Earl referred to above (presumably able, despite the image of the eternally impoverished Scottish aristocracy, to afford the odd bawbee), was not alone in not thinking the operation worth the money. (The recording incidentally was separate from the baptismal activity which appears to have gone ahead undisturbed). Governments had at various stages imposed stamp payments on such entries and these, as with all taxes, had an immediate effect of a deterrent—an effect which may or may not have worn off as time went by. The records for

Kirkcaldy at the end of the 18th century bewail one newly introduced payment and gave it as the reason for a sharp drop in the number of entries.

This is a far cry from the post-1855 situation where the state took on full responsibility for ensuring total registration.

In three other respects, the old parochial registers show marked and (for the ancestor-hunter) frustrating differences from the newer records. Firstly, there was no standard to which clerks were expected to conform. The result is that the information varies considerably from year to year, from parish to parish (as indeed does the quality of writing and degree of preservation). Secondly, as these were church registers, they set out to record not so much births as baptisms (although the birth date was often given), not so much marriages as banns and weddings, not so much deaths as burials.

The third and greatest difference lies in the fact that civil registration brought with it in 1855 a responsibility for the care, preservation, storing and indexing of the records. Before 1855, this was a matter of individual practice and bent. This is reflected in the lists of Old Parochial Records held by the Registrar-General. Many parishes are defective in certain years, ranging from enormous gaps of decades at a time to small periods. Some parishes have little or no representation at all. Scotland has done much to preserve these records, to maintain them in a single building, to make them available to the public researchers. For over a century the actual original documents were available to researchers, but constant and increasing use threatens the old records and impairs their legibility. Plans are now well advanced to withdraw the actual documents from normal public consultation and replace them with microfilm copies. Just how useful these records will be to you depends, however, not on the care and attention given to the documents today, but that lavished on them before 1855—plus a great element of luck as far as survival is concerned.

Pauline Brydon tracks down the posthumous birth of Euphemia Brydon—and pinpoints more closely the death of the father

Once again, the first thing you want to know is just how do you plug into this vast hoard of 4000 volumes of handwritten registers from not much fewer than a thousand Scottish parishes, ranging in age from the baptisms and banns in the parish of Errol in Perthshire in 1553 to the registers compiled on the eve of 1855, when the responsibility passed to the state?

The first thing to understand as far as the "plugging-in" operation is concerned is that the rules have changed yet again. In the case of the statutory civil registers, the "unit" was the individual—let's say, William Forbes Miller. In the case of the census returns, the "unit" was an address—let's say, Sauchiehall Street, Glasgow or Cumbernauld Village. Now, in the case of the Old Parochial Records (hereafter OPRs), the "unit" is the parish. Without that information, there is no way into the records which will lead you to the person or family you are after. To know the name of a person and not the parish is like trying to find the telephone number of someone when you only know his Christian name.

By this stage you will have had some idea of which parish you are going to be playing in:

1. The Census returns from 1851 onwards included a note of the place in which the individual was born. In some cases this would have been given as the parish itself, in others perhaps the name of a large town or city, or even (and you are going to curse your forebears for being so lazy) only the county.
2. The Births, Marriages and Deaths in the years immediately after 1855 will have given you some clue to the places in which a family lived.
3. You may even have had detailed information from the Bonus Year entries of 1855.

No matter what the state of play, you have to come to some conclusion about the parishes to be searched. If you have no idea of where to look at this stage, you must take steps to identify some of the later census returns in order to find the

Reference

OPR	FORFAR (contd)		
	310. MONIFIETH		
310/1	B 1562-1620	M 1560-1620	D -
310/2	B 1621-49	M 1621-49	D -
310/3	B 1649-1780	M -	D -
310/4	B 1781-1819	M -	D -
310/5	B -	M 1649-1819	D 1659-1804
310/6	B 1820-54	M 1820-54	D 1833-54
	311. MONIKIE*		
311/1	B 1613-67	M 1613-37	D 1613-60
311/2	B 1668-1717	M 1668-1717	D 1703-17
311/3	B 1719-1819	M 1717-1819	D 1783-1819
311/4	B -	M -	D 1717-33
311/5	B 1820-54	M 1820-54	D 1820
311/6	B -	M -	D 1842-54 †

*See Appendix under reference CH2/499

†From the original in the Scottish Record Office, ref CH2/499/6

information. If, for example, you were unable to find anyone at the address on an 1857 certificate when the census was taken in 1861, you must try and find the birth of a brother or sister nearer the census year to help you find the new address. If you have only the details of the 1841 Census (which did *not* give place of birth) go and see if there was anyone at that address for the 1851 Census (which did).

If the worst comes to the worst, you will have to gamble. If the family were all living in Lanark in the 1850s, then try there for the births. The other facts which you will have noted from the census returns and from such as the Marriage and Death Certificates will have been the approximate ages, and this information combined with the possible parishes will enable you to begin your search.

The first line into the OPRs is to be found in two small volumes listing the parishes for which the Registrar-General holds records (they actually belong to the Church of Scotland). At the end of each volume is an alphabetical list of parishes indicating the reference number under which they are grouped—and this will in turn let you know which of the two volumes to use.

The page opposite shows you a typical treatment for a parish. As you see, the Registrar-General holds records for Births, Marriages and Deaths in the parish for the years shown. The reference number in the first column identifies the book containing the records. When you have decided which years and records you wish to consult you can fill in the details on a requisition slip.

One important point before I go on to discuss the type of material you are likely to find. For the most part these OPRs are unindexed. If you are lucky, you will find that the clerk kept a rough running index (that is, grouping all "A's in one section, all "B"s on another page, etc.) which will not be in strict alphabetical order but which helps. If you are very lucky, some kind soul will have produced a fine typescript index (generally in the larger towns) and if you are very, very lucky you will find there is actually a fully comprehensive

INDEX for 1836.

published index. A series of reference marks on the two-volume index will show you when such indexes exist. Where they do, use them! The Genealogical Society of Utah, linked with the Church of Christ's Latter Day Saints, has started work on preparing a comprehensive county-by-county index of the Old Parochial Registers dealing with Baptisms and Marriages, and the General Register Office will invest in a set when it becomes available; but this is a mammoth task and will take some years to complete.

BIRTHS AND BAPTISMS

These were invariably the record of an actual baptism in the church—and as we are talking about records from the Church of Scotland, this limits us to members of that Church, although the various Presbyterian variations were usually included with the main-line Church.

Aside from the basic problem of OPRs (sheer survival) we have the additional ones of not every birth being accompanied by a baptism (although pressures, religious and social, did their best to see that it was). Sometimes there was a shortage of ready cash to defer, perhaps indefinitely, the religious ceremony. Sometimes, you will find out that four or five brothers and sisters are baptised at once, the arrival of the latest one providing the occasion for getting them all done. You can see what this will do to your searches if you are looking for a baptismal entry for William Miller whom you know to have been born in 1850/1, when in fact he was baptised along with three little Millers in 1854! Perhaps a new minister came in and decided to have a baptism drive. Generally speaking, I get the impression that the pressures to get the child baptised were stronger on a family in a tightly-knit rural community than on a family in one of the teeming urban centres.

The information given does not vary to any great extent.

January 1791

Pomarium January twenty sixth one thousand seven hundred & Ninety one years was born **Alexander Mac Farlane** Lawfull Son to Thomas Mac Farlane Weaver in Pomarium & Janet Glass his spouse and baptized the Thirteenth day of February said year by Mr Jedediah Aitkman Minister of the Dissenting Congregation in Perth.

Upper Friartown January twenty seventh one thousand seven hundred & Ninety one years was born **John Barclay** Lawfull Son to William Barclay Servant to James Buchan Farmer of Kildinny & Friertown & Margaret Sharp his spouse & Baptized the Sixth day of February said year by Mr Robert Forsyth Minister of the Associate Congregation at Craigend.

Perth the twenty seventh day of January one thousand seven hundred & Ninety one years was born **Jean Donaldson** Lawfull Daughter to Robert Donaldson Mason in Perth & Margaret Peddie his spouse and Baptized the Thirtieth day of January said year by the Reverend Mr David Black Minister of the Gospel at Saint Madoes.

Perth the Twenty seventh day of January one thousand seven hundred & Ninety one years was born **Jean Miller** Lawfull Daughter to Walter Miller Wright in Perth & Mary Young his spouse but not Baptized her Parents being Annabaptistes.

Perth the Twenty eight day of January one thousand seven hundred & Ninety one years was born **Charles Miller** Lawfull Son to Peter Miller Plaisterer in Perth & Margaret Hepburn his spouse and Baptized the third day of February said year by Mr Richard Black Minister of the Associate Congregation in Perth.

The name of the father and the mother invariably appears (usually with the mother's maiden name), the date of the birth as well as the baptism is stated and, in the earlier years, a particularly important feature is the listing of witnesses, generally two, one for each side of the family. In view of the sparse nature of information in the OPRs generally, these names can often provide confirmation of a relationship or reveal the existence of other members of the family. A typical combination of witnesses might be brothers of husband and of wife, fathers of husband and of wife. They are usually furnished with some details about their occupations and location. A man may be described as "farmer of such and such a farm," or "merchant in such a port."

A feature in the birth entries which should be brought to the attention of any susceptible readers is the preoccupation, especially in the more rustic areas, with legitimacy. Where necessary, the phrase "born in fornication" is used without hesitation and, in contrast to later registrations, the name of the erring father is invariably given. You must remember that basically we are dealing with the records of the Church in a community, and the moral role is one which plays a part even in the chronicling of births.

The occasional oddity will come up in these birth records. The existence of foundlings was widespread and the task of naming the child and integrating him/her into the community lay with the Church. The birth records reflect this concern. Great care is taken with naming systems (readers of *Oliver Twist* will remember that he was called "Twist" because they had reached "T" in the alphabet). Many were given the name "Kirk" or "Church" if they were abandoned in the porch of the church. Others even had Christian names pinned to their clothes when found. Gerald Hamilton-Edwards in his excellent *In Search of Scottish Ancestry* gives the example of the foundling at Coupar Angus who was promptly named "Angus Coupar." For all the colourful nature of this type of entry, it will invariably mean the end of one line as far as the genealogist is concerned.

May 13th 1732

John Comb & Marg^t Gillespie

Betwixt John Comb in this Parish and Marg^t Gillespie in the Parish of Dalmeny gave half a Crown to the poor in pledge of marriage.

May 13th 1732

Tho Wilson & Anne Comb

Betwixt Thomas Wilson and Anne Comb both in this parish gave three Shillings to the poor in pledge of Marriage. maried june 16th.

May 19th 1732

Ja: Hastie & Janet Gogar

Betwixt James Hastie in this parish & Janet Gogar in the Westkirk parish gave two Shillings to ye poor in pledge of marriage married at west kirk.

May 19th 1732

Ja: Dowie & Agnes Napper

Betwixt James Dowie in this parish & Agnes Napper in the parish of Cramond gave half a Crown to ye poor in pledge of marriage married at Currie

julie 7th 1732

Robt Hutton & Jan: Paris

Betwixt Robert Hutton in this parish and Janet Parish in the West kirk parish gave two shillings to ye poor in pledge of marriage. married at west kirk julie 20th 1732.

August 5th 1732

James Dundass & Elis: Cleghorn

Betwixt James Dundass baxter in Edinr and Elisabeth Cleghorn Daughter to the deceast Wm Cleghorn tennent in Granton gave a Crown to ye poor in pledge of marriage married 17th instant.

October 29th 1732

Jo: Colvin & Marg^t Sibbald

Betwixt John Colvin in this parish and Marg^t Sibald in Kirkliston parish gave two Shillings Sterling in pledge of marriage married Novr 16th

Sometimes you will find a clue to the naming of the legitimate offspring. In Dundee, one clerk instigated an efficient columnar system which simplified the recording of baptisms and included a column headed "After whom the child is named." In view of the rigid naming patterns of Scottish families (see Appendix II), this is an invaluable extra.

In other cases, the entry itself will enlighten you. For example, I was puzzled at the existence of a Walker Dundas in a family which had never used the name Walker before, and where there was no evidence of its being brought in from the mother's side. When I found the actual baptismal entry for 22nd April 1759, I saw that the witnesses included a Mr Walker, surgeon. Here was an example of another quaint custom of naming the child after the doctor, when it was his first delivery or when there was particular reason to thank him—for a difficult birth, perhaps.

BANNS AND MARRIAGES

In the case of marriages, the rigid distinction between Church of Scotland and the other Churches was blurred. The reading of banns had a social as well as a religious significance and it was not uncommon to find the established Church mixing the functions. Banns relating to a Catholic couple could easily be read in a Protestant church and even a note made of the actual marriage taking place before a Roman Catholic priest. For the most part, however, we are again talking about the national Church's religious ceremonies rather than the systematic maintenance of a society's records.

The great pressure on the marriage being recorded was an obvious one—and goes some way to explaining that you will often come across families whose marriages have been religiously (in all senses of the word) recorded, but where there are no traces of any baptismal records. In the pre-1855 communities, the Church's concern with morals focussed

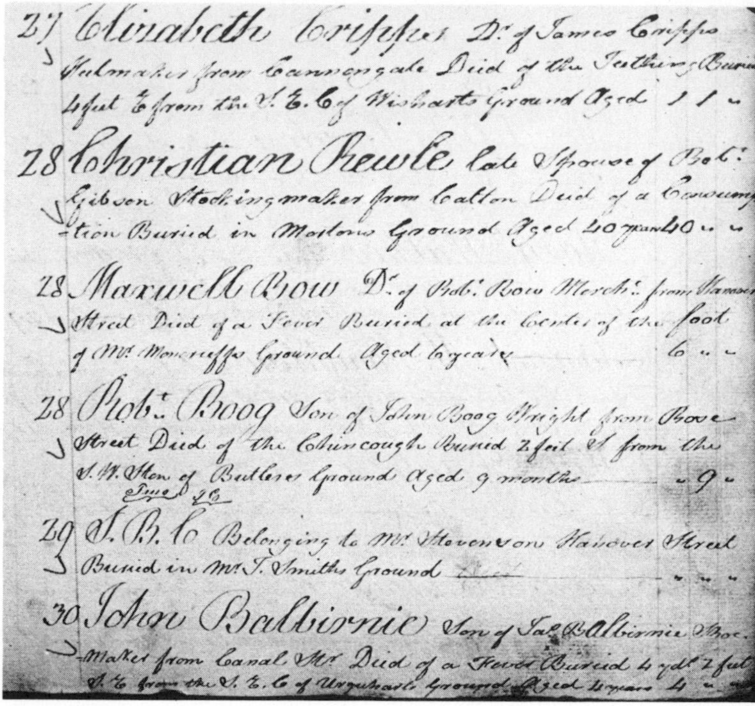

27 Elizabeth Crispses Dr. of James Crisps Hatmaker from Canongate Died of the Teething Buried 4 feet E from the S.E.C of Wisharts Ground Aged 1 1 ..

28 Christian Rewle late Spouse of Robt. Gibson Stockingmaker from Calton Died of a Consumption Buried in Marlows Ground Aged 40 years 40 .. ..

28 Maxwell Bow Dr. of Robt. Bow Mercht. from Hanover Street Died of a Fever Buried at the Center of the foot of Mr. Moncreiffs Ground Aged 6 years 6 .. ..

28 Robt. Boog Son of John Boog Wright from Rose Street Died of the Chincough Buried 2 feet S from the S.W. Ston of Butlers Ground Aged 9 months .. 9 ..

29 S.B.C Belonging to Mr. Stevenson Hanover Street Buried in Mr. T. Smiths Ground .. .. ..

30 John Balbirnie Son of Jas. Balbirnie Boo-Maker from Canal St. Died of a Fever Buried 4 yds 2 feet S.E from the S.E.C of Urquharts Ground Aged 4 years 4 ..

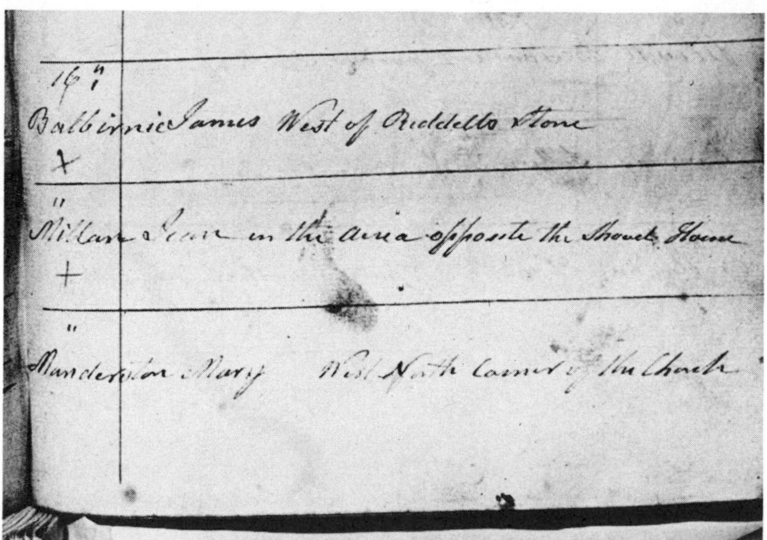

16"

Balbirnie James West of Riddells Stone

+

"

Millar Jean in the area opposite the Shovel House

+

"

Manderston Mary West North Corner of the Church

very sharply on sexual morals—after all, lust is the most apparent of the Seven Deadly Sins as far as its results are concerned! One can debate about Sloth and Envy, Pride and even Gluttony, but Lust comes to light. And the only evidence you could produce in your defence was the marriage lines. Look at the records of the Sessions and you will find, time and time again, the deacons insisting on seeing the marriage lines as proof that there was no sin.

The information given in the records of banns and marriages is disappointingly slight. Sometimes you will find little more than the name of the two partners. When it is necessary to name parents, you will find this is usually restricted to the father of the bride. While this is a useful pointer to the next stage—an extra lug on the jigsaw piece in the case of the wife—the absence of this information in the case of the husband means that the only link with the earlier generation is through the birth/baptismal entry (there is rarely if ever a mention of parentage in the case of the burial of a man as opposed to that of a child).

DEATHS AND BURIALS

If the records of births and marriages are far from satisfactory, the situation when it comes to deaths is even more likely to cause frustration. These records are basically not religious records in the sense that baptisms and banns are. They are records kept by the people who run the graveyards—usually in earlier times the responsibility of the church, but often, especially later in the period, people charged specifically with looking after the large urban graveyards.

Sometimes, you have to rely on records which are not of interments but accounts of people borrowing the mort-cloth used in the ceremony. Even where records are well kept, the variation from one graveyard to the next is extraordinary.

Take these two examples from Edinburgh graveyards which are actually within sight of each other. The entries were made in the same decade and refer, I think, to two brothers.

In the first case, the details, beside being splendidly written, include the name of the father, his occupation and address, the age of person who has died, the cause of death and full details of the location of the grave. The information allowed me to fit the child confidently into the family history.

In the second case, the only information given is the name of the person who has died and the date of the interment. Only the unusual name and the fact that I have records of the birth and apprenticeship of a James Balbirnie in 1783 and 1799 give me any defence for tentatively putting this down as the date of death of the person in my records.

Often the gravestones give more information than the written records. Indeed in many cases there are no written records. The logging of the grave inscriptions is therefore an important dimension to the maintaining of Scotland's records. This has been painstakingly undertaken by a number of Scotland's genealogists, notably by Mr John Fowler Mitchell and his wife, Sheila. As a result of the work done by them and like-minded Scots, there are many typewritten folders carrying valuable information from these "stone books"—and not just those inscriptions relating to the high and powerful. A superb collection of these transcripts from the length and breadth of Scotland is available for study in the library of New Register House, in the room where you will be studing the OPRs. Their value lies not only in sparing you a trip to Inverness (either by showing what is on the family tomb or by telling you there isn't one there), but also in recording many inscriptions which are succumbing day by day to pollution and Scotland's high rainfall.

The OPRs are erratic, frustrating, difficult and at times the writing can be positively mind-boggling. Sometimes you are called upon to resort to viewing them through microfilm equipment—a procedure which may bother you at first but which soon slips into place.

For all that, they provide, through the occasional flash of an entry, an enormous amount of satisfaction. Perhaps they don't provide the wealth of data which comes from the post-1855 variety, but there is something more than a fact when you read, for example, in the quaintly penned records of Cramond church that two forebears in 1732, "James Dundass, baxter, and Elizabeth Cleghorn, daughter of the deceased William Cleghorn, tenant in Granton, gave a crown to the poor in pledge of marriage."

What can you expect to achieve in a week at New Register House?

Two real case-histories underline the problems and the potential of a week's work among the records

After listening patiently to a catalogue of the work I have done on my wife's family tree, a friend asked the simple question: "How long did it take you to put all of this together?" I was hurtled into a well-oiled answer, emphasising the ease of the chase, the glories of the Scottish records and the spontaneity of my own deductions, before I came to an abrupt halt. I realised that I was committing what seems to be a prevalent sin among ancestor-hunters, and in particular writers on the subject: I was forgetting the realities of the time-scales in my enthusiasm for the end result. Look at any book on genealogy and you will see just what I mean: the writer condenses twenty years' search into a single book and forgets the months of search which were rewarded with but a single name or date, the days poring over records, the undergrowth of dead-ends.

The lesson stuck—and when soon afterwards I came to write a series for The Royal Bank of Scotland's staff publication *Countertalk*, which was to lead to this book, I determined to avoid this pitfall. I looked for two willing guinea-pigs who would, from a base of only a small amount of information on their forebears, set off on the search. The project was to be confined to the records kept at New Register House (the statutory civil records since 1855, the census returns and the Old Parochial Records), because this represents a fund of information which will be applicable to nearly every searcher, because the methods would again be relevant not only to the two people but also to the readers of the article, and because the "scaffolding" built up from these records is essential to any real success in the wider records of Scotland.

The two "volunteers," who figure in many of the photographs in this book, were Pauline Brydon, who was responsible among other things for the Bank's Free Film Show service which has proved such a boon to a span of Scottish clubs from Women's Institutes to Young Farmers' groups; and Bob Leitch, who was at that time (early 1980) assistant Public Relations Officer at the Bank. Originally I thought to cover the east and west coasts, as Pauline had been brought up on the south edge of Edinburgh and Bob to the south of Glasgow. As things turned out, within a generation we were back to Edinburgh in both cases! I owe a lot to both of them for their very willing co-operation in the search and their permission to use our findings in this book.

CASE HISTORY ONE

Pauline Brydon is extremely methodical and produces as our starting point the death certificate of her grandfather, James Brydon, originally obtained for insurance purposes.

This tells us that James, a retired stevedore, had been married to Margaret Reynolds, had been born on 17 March 1894 and had died on 27 March 1969. His deceased parents are given as James Bryden, carter, and Margaret Bryden, m.s. (maiden surname) Stewart. It also indicates that the spelling of the name had changed from Bry*den* (his father's name) to Bry*don*. This is a symptom of the modern bureaucratic concern for standardised spelling which had little or no equivalent in the nineteenth century. We shall indeed find that his father had earlier been known as Bry*don* which brings us right back to where we started—and gives an early reminder of the problems of spelling in our work!

This single document enables Pauline to produce this rough chart immediately:

(If she had not been able to lay her hands on that death certificate, we would have had to get that same information from the original held at New Register House).

We go to New Register House and pay a fee to allow us to inspect the indexes to the statutory records, the census returns and the OPRs. Initially, it is the post-1855 Births, Marriages and Deaths that concern us.

We have a choice of tactics: we can either look for the birth certificate of the grandfather (we know from his death certificate that this was in 1894) in order to find the date of his parents' marriage or we can try and bypass that stage by looking directly for the marriage. This is always a case of personal judgement, but here we have a fairly distinctive combination of names as far as the parents are concerned, so we try to find their marriage directly from the indexes. (This is a bit of a gamble especially when you realise that marriages in Scotland between 1861 and 1871 produced on average 4.51 legitimate births, and that if you have caught the tail-end of a large family you could have a long backward trek to the original marriage. But here we risk it, encouraged perhaps by the fact that the son bears the same name as his father and is likely to be the first male offspring).

We are looking for the marriage certificate of James Bryden and Margaret Stewart. We pick one of the pair, James Bryden, on the grounds that there would be fewer James Brydens than Margaret Stewarts in the records. Looking at the Marriage Indexes, Males for 1893, we draw a blank; 1892, a blank; 1891, a blank; 1890, eureka!—a marriage entry for James Bryden, at the registration district of South Leith, entry number 118. Before arranging to see this entry, we carry out a check: if he is our man, then there must be a corresponding entry for Margaret Stewart. So we check the 1890 index for female marriages and find Margaret Stewart, also South Leith 118. It looks as if we have the right pair.

Now to get to see that actual entry. As we mentioned, this is a privilege granted by the Registrar-General and not something we can insist on as a right. We study a chart on the wall of the main public room and find that the reference for Leith South is 692/2. (Be very careful in checking this—some districts vary throughout the period). We now have all that we need to identify the entry.

We put down our name on a list kept on the counter and wait for the call. Five minutes or so later (in the summer it would have taken us longer perhaps), it is our turn and one of the attendants takes us up to the first floor of the circular building (Marriages) and brings us the actual book in which the marriage details were originally entered.

We copy down the details in pencil (a pen in these premises is as welcome as a lamb chop at a vegetarians' conference!) and we make use of the forms we had already drawn out at home (see page 27).

The basic details are: James Brydon was a carter, aged 21, who lived at 13 Gordon Street, Leith (the port for Edinburgh) and his parents were William Brydon and Jennet Brydon *m.s.* MacQueen.

His bride was Margaret Stewart, aged 21, who lived around

the corner from him at 24 Ferrier Street. Her parents were Thomas Stewart, boilermaker, and Janet Stewart, *m.s.* Morris.

This document enables Pauline to progress another generation and to add to her chart the following lines:

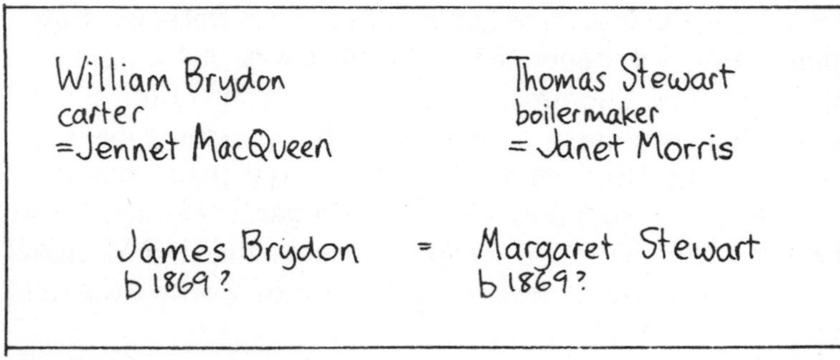

We have been able to put in some tentative birth dates for the couple from the marriage certificate ages, but we cannot take any ages as absolutely accurate.

The information has given us the names of four of Pauline's great-great-grandparents and we pick the Brydon pair again and set off in search of another marriage entry. Again, we try to bypass the birth entry for James (around 1869) and look for a marriage entry. We stick with William Brydon (as hunting for Jennet MacQueen would bring us into the complications of having to look up both Mc and Mac in the indexes) and go backwards from 1869 through the Male Marriages. We have to go back a long way and are approaching the cut-off date of 1855 when we find in the 1856 index volume a marriage for William Brydon (and a corresponding one for Jennet MacQueen). This has taken us a long time and in retrospect we might have been better off finding the date of the marriage from their son's birth certificate!

The same procedure again—note the year (1856), the district of South Leith (692/2 again), and the entry number (124). We put down our name on the counter list and wait to be called again. When there is an attendant free, we are off again, telling him that we want a marriage entry for 1856, for 692/2. He locates the book and opens it at the entry number we require.

The couple were married at Summerfield House on 3 October 1856 and both were shown as living in Redfords Close, Leith. William's parents are given as Thomas Brydon and Margaret Brydon, *m.s.* Taylor and Jennet's as Alexander MacQueen and Jennet MacQueen, *m.s.* McDonald.

We have taken another step backwards to Pauline's great-great-grandparents, but we have reached the great divide of 1855.

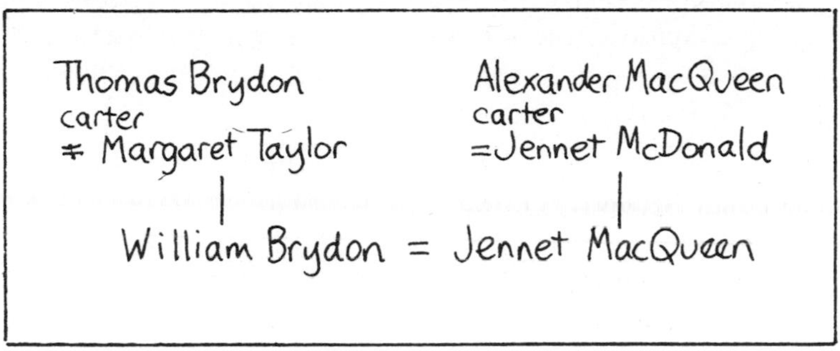

We pick out Thomas Brydon as our point of investigation and note, from the marriage certificate of his son, that he is not shown as deceased. Moreover, a Thomas Brydon has signed the register as witness. So we assume that he is still alive. We can find out his parents from his death certificate, so we spend a long time looking through the death certificate indexes for a Thomas Brydon who would fit the bill. We give up this approach and leave the post-1855 records for the census returns: perhaps we can find some guidelines there.

Now in the 1856 marriage certificate, the groom William is shown living at Redfords Close, Leith. So we decide to see if we can trace him (and maybe his parents) living at that address at the time of the 1851 Census. We go upstairs to the library of New Register House. Fortunately, we are outside the really busy period and they are able to find a seat for us. We look up the index for the 1851 Census returns—Leith, included in the Edinburgh returns, has a street index to help us. We look up Redfords Close and find that the returns are carried in a number of enumeration books, bound in a number of volumes. It looks like being a long street—and street numbering is no use, as we don't have a number to go for.

We fill in a requisition slip indicating our seat number and showing (CEN 1851) that we require returns for the 1851 Census and (692/2) Leith books for the numbers shown for Redfords Close.

As feared, it is a very long street, teeming with people. The writing is spidery, the ink an erratic brown. Eventually, we find, after a long time peering at the Name columns: Brydon, Book 25, Entry 75. It reads:

Margaret Brydon, widow, head of family, 31 years old
William Brydon, son, aged 13, scholar
Thomas, son, aged 11, scholar
Margaret, daughter, 11, scholar
Janet, daughter, 9, scholar
James, son, 5, scholar
Euphemia, daughter, 2

All are shown to have been born in the same area (Leith).

We are given a very full picture of the family, but one item of information comes as a complete surprise: the father, Thomas, is dead! Obviously, there was an error in that 1856 marriage certificate in not indicating that the groom's father was deceased—and the Thomas Brydon signing it must have been the groom's brother, shown in this census return as an eleven-year-old schoolboy.

We are not too enamoured over this omission—it has cost us a lot of time looking for the post-1855 death of a man we now know to have been dead in 1851!

We can tentatively fill in some birth dates, bearing in mind what I have already said about the reliability or otherwise of these stated ages. A typical example is William, here shown as 13 years old but appearing five years later on his marriage certificate as 21 years old.

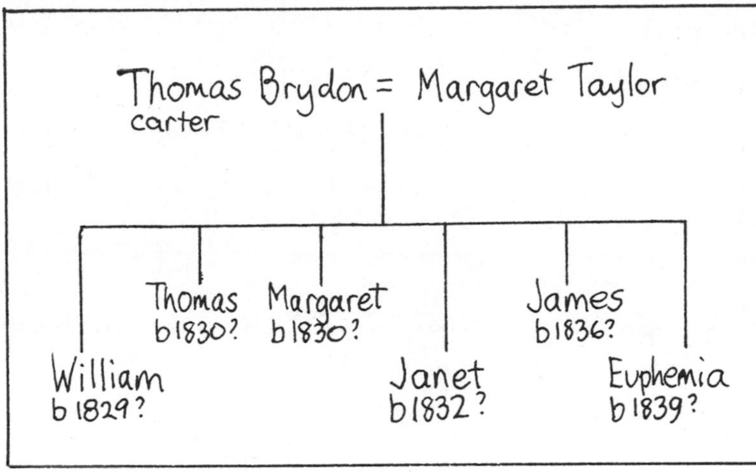

One little glimpse into life in Leith at this time is provided by the large number of entries for Redfords Close, where a woman's occupation column carries the note, "Has a mangle." Clearly, in these pre-tumble-drier days, capital investment in a mangle could show some financial return!

The civil registration and the census returns have pointed to one fact for the next stage of our search: the family seems to have been well established in the parish of South Leith and this is where we must look for information in the Old Parochial Records.

Again the procedure changes. We look up the master list of OPRs held in New Register House and see that there is a fairly complete collection of records for South Leith between 1800 and 1855. We take Euphemia as the youngest of the children shown in the 1851 Census returns and look for a possible birth entry around 1849. We request the volume containing birth records for South Leith for this year, indicating on our requisition slip that we want OPR (Old

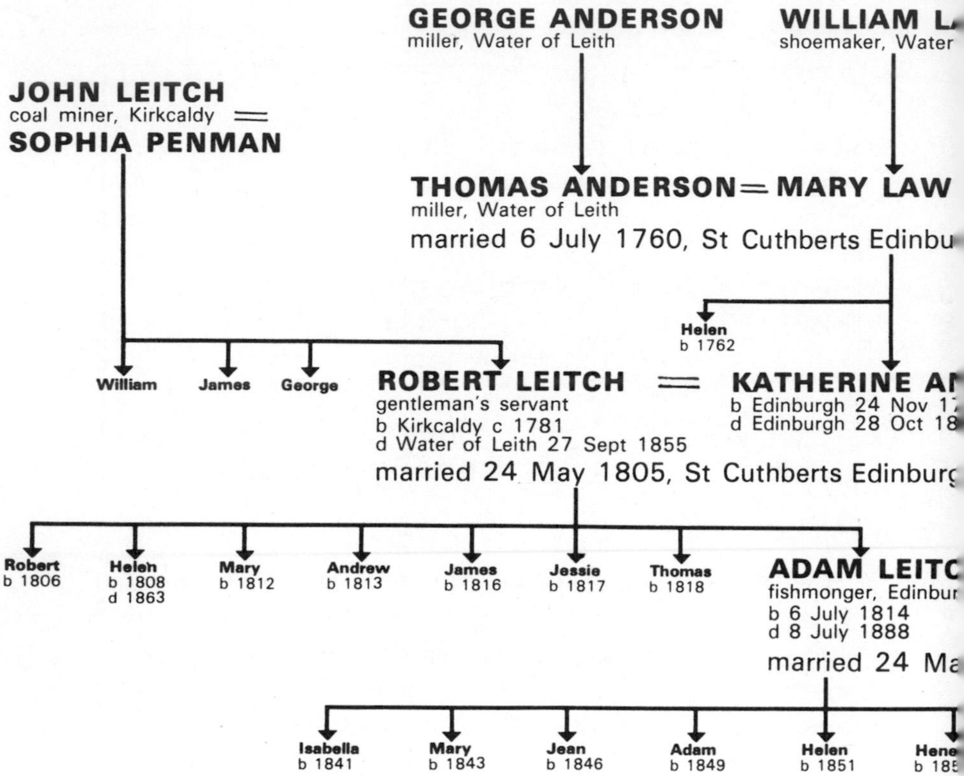

The family tree produced by Bob Leitch after his week in New Register House

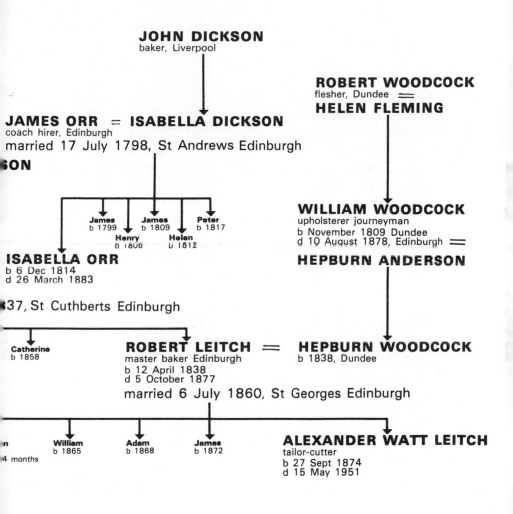

JOHN DICKSON
baker, Liverpool

ROBERT WOODCOCK
flesher, Dundee =
HELEN FLEMING

JAMES ORR = **ISABELLA DICKSON**
coach hirer, Edinburgh
married 17 July 1798, St Andrews Edinburgh

SON

James b 1799
Henry b 1806
James b 1809
Helen b 1812
Peter b 1817

ISABELLA ORR
b 6 Dec 1814
d 26 March 1883

WILLIAM WOODCOCK
upholsterer journeyman
b November 1809 Dundee
d 10 August 1878, Edinburgh =
HEPBURN ANDERSON

37, St Cuthberts Edinburgh

Catherine b 1858

ROBERT LEITCH = **HEPBURN WOODCOCK**
master baker Edinburgh
b 12 April 1838
d 5 October 1877

b 1838, Dundee

married 6 July 1860, St Georges Edinburgh

n
4 months

William b 1865
Adam b 1868
James b 1872

ALEXANDER WATT LEITCH
tailor-cutter
b 27 Sept 1874
d 15 May 1951

Parochial Records) 692/2 (South Leith), the volume containing the year 1849.

This time we are in luck, finding a well-kept book, beautifully written and with the surnames clearly picked out in each page. We find an entry for Euphemia Brydon and find that she was born posthumously to Thomas Brydon and his wife Margaret Taylor.

This pins down the death of Thomas Brydon, but is the last piece of luck Pauline is to find in her search. The rest of our allocated time is spent trying to track down other entries relating to the Brydon family in the OPRs of South Leith. No mention in baptisms, banns or burials! We turn to the adjoining parish of North Leith—with similar results.

We return to the security of the post-1855 records and manage to tie up a few odds and ends, relating to deaths and offspring of people already identified in our chart, but no lead to extend our tree backwards.

The census records prove particularly elusive. None of the people in our chart seem to figure in trade directories and the addresses given on births, marriages and deaths near census dates turn out not to apply when we come to look at the census returns. A long, long search—with little to show for it after the early successes. We certainly have a few long shots which we can pursue later, but in general Pauline's search has had disappointing results.

CASE HISTORY TWO

Bob Leitch produces a case history which is in many instances the exact opposite of Pauline's. Whereas she started precisely and finished up with a misleading error in the records and complete lack of success in the OPRs, Bob starts with a considerable stutter and finishes up with a jack-pot—an 1855 death—followed up by a fine run in the OPRs.

The initial stutter comes about because Bob sets off with the wrong Christian name for his grandfather—a not uncommon failure in instances where someone is recalling a grandparent who died when one was young! After some fruitless delving in the indexes, Bob phones his mother and comes back with the real Christian name: and from that moment he never looks back—if that's the right phrase.

Bob starts off then with only a name and an approximate date, giving him a starting point something like this:

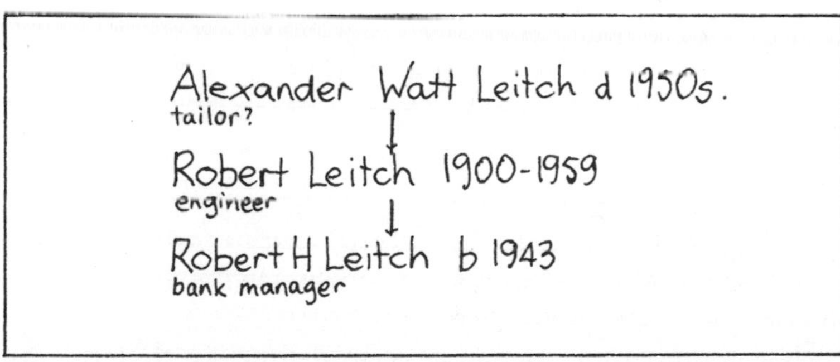

We have the advantage of a not-too-common surname, Leitch—and a fine and distinctive combination of Christian names, Alexander Watt—to help us get off to a good start.

We look through the indexes for Male Deaths around the early 1950s and find for 1952 a death entry for Alexander Watt Leitch for St Andrews Edinburgh 296. We go through the routine—look up St Andrews Edinburgh on the wall chart and note the reference number 685/2. We put our name down and soon are taken up to the second floor (Deaths), feeling sprightly on our first ascent but trying to remember that the helpful assistant has probably done this a dozen times already!

He shows us the entry and we copy down the details on the headed pages of our note-book. In amongst the usual facts we find that Bob's grandfather was a master tailor/cutter, that he died at the age of 77 at Leslie Place in Edinburgh and, key facts for our investigation, his parents were master-baker Robert Leitch and Hepburn Woodcock. (We note in passing that he was married to Margaret MacKenzie, a fact to be stored away on his personal sheet as the subject of a later search perhaps).

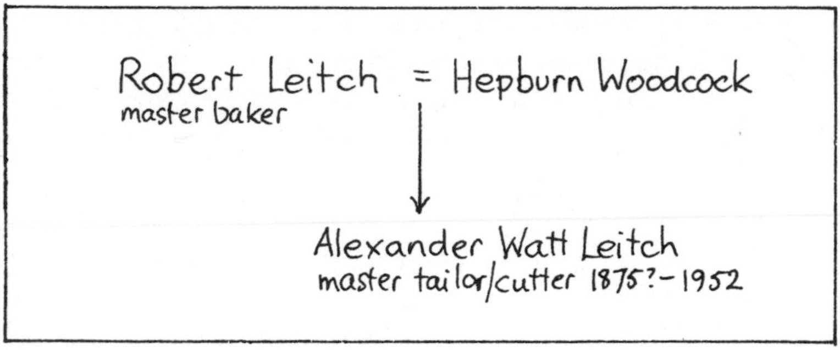

We are in luck. You don't get many names as distinctive as Hepburn Woodcock—and hers is obviously the name we can pick for our index searching.

That combination of names is so distinctive that we can bypass looking for Alexander Watt Leitch's birth certificate to find the date of his parents' marriage and look backwards from his approximate birth date (1874) for a marriage. We go back quite a way (to 1860) before coming across a Hepburn Woodcock in the Female Marriages. Even with such an unusual name, we still check that there is an equivalent partner (Robert Leitch) in the 1860 Male Marriages to show that this really is *our* pair.

Through the routine—and we are looking at the actual entry once again.

> Robert Leitch, a baker, aged 22, lived at 14 Bedford Street, Edinburgh, the son of Adam Leitch, a fishmonger, and Isabella Orr. He married Hepburn Woodcock of 3 Leggats Land, Stockbridge, 22-year-old daughter of William Woodcock, an upholsterer, and Hepburn Anderson.

This enables Bob to add a couple of blocks to the next generation band.

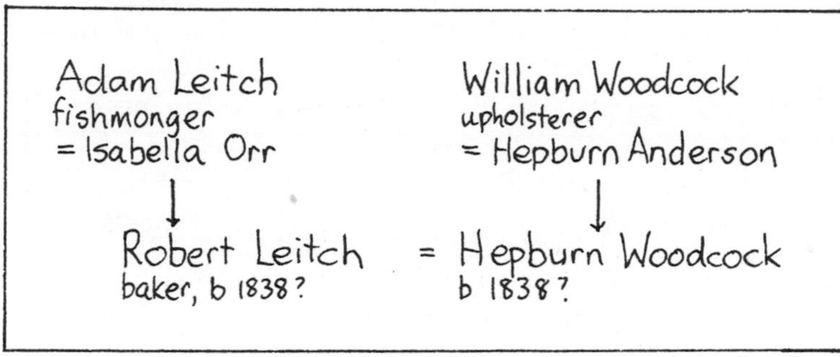

From the age of the groom, it is deduced that he, Robert Leitch, was born around 1838. His parents' marriage would not therefore appear in the post-1855 records. Neither of them, however, is shown to be dead at the time of his marriage in 1860, so it is worth trying (despite our chastening experiences of a similar situation in the case of Pauline!) to find the death of the father, Adam Leitch. The name is unusual enough to avoid too many false alarms—and the family seems to be localised in Edinburgh. We work forward on Male Deaths from 1860 and it takes us a long and hefty spell at the large volumes before we find in the index for 1888 an entry for the death of an Adam Leitch.

By this time, the indexes are showing the age of deceased people. This man is shown as 73 years old—so we are in the right area. We go through the procedure—a note of the registration district code, a name on the waiting list and soon we are up on the second floor among the Death certificates.

A quick check at the occupation, and it seems certain he is ours—his occupation is given as "fishmonger." We shall be looking for absolute confirmation at a later stage, but this seems enough to go on at the moment.

Key facts among those entered on our notepad are: he was married to Isabella Orr (now deceased) and his parents are given as Robert Leitch, butler, and Catherine Anderson.

So Bob can now tag on quite a few branches to Adam Leitch:

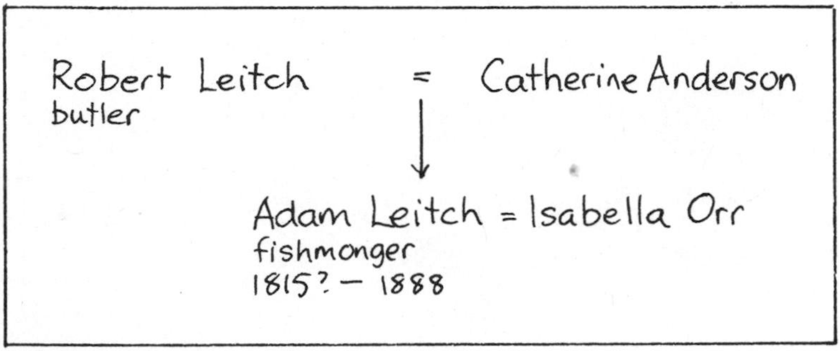

This is where we have an unexpected turn of luck. Before going on to either the census returns or the OPRs, we decide to see if we can find a Robert Leitch, that butler (top left) dying after 1855. We look at the 1855 returns—and there, sure enough, in Edinburgh is a Robert Leitch! This is the great jackpot year—can it possibly be our Robert Leitch, the father of Adam Leitch (1815-1888)?

We chance our arm and ask to see the entry. It is a Robert Leitch of the right age. And he was married to a Catherine Anderson—he must be our man. But he is not a butler—his occupation is given as labourer! And in this great year of 1855, we have the added bonus of a list of all his children, living and dead! We look through them for a sign of our Adam Leitch. Among the seven children, no son called Adam. Disappointment—and we are about to close the book when we notice that the informant is . . . Adam Leitch, fishmonger and son to the deceased. A son who had left his own name off the list of children! We have found our man—beyond a shadow of doubt—and learnt the lesson of peering at every column for the smallest scrap of information.

Bob's bull's-eye of an 1855 death certificate is in fact a valuable one indeed. Here is some of the wealth of data carried by that single entry:

- Robert Leitch died on 27 September 1855. The place was given as the Water of Leith—not, in fact, a drowning in the water that runs through Edinburgh but the name given then to the delightful village now known as Dean Village.
- He had died of paralysis which he had had for eight years (this often refers to the effects of a stroke).
- He had been married to Katherine Anderson (slightly different spelling of the Christian name but confirmation of the information given on their son's (Adam's) death certificate). Katherine was still alive at the time of Robert's death.
- Robert was 74 years old and had lived at his present address for 50 years. He had been born at Kirkcaldy in Fife.
- He was buried in Dean Cemetery.
- His father was John Leitch, coal miner, and his mother, Sophia Penman.
- He and Katherine had had the following children (as at 1855), Robert (dead), Helen (47 years old), Mary (43), Andrew (42), James (dead), Jessie (dead), Thomas (dead) and of course Adam, confirmed by the informant's details but left out of the list.

That information provides a suitable climax to the searches among the post-1855 records, allowing us to add a lot of detail to the Robert Leitch corner of our tree.

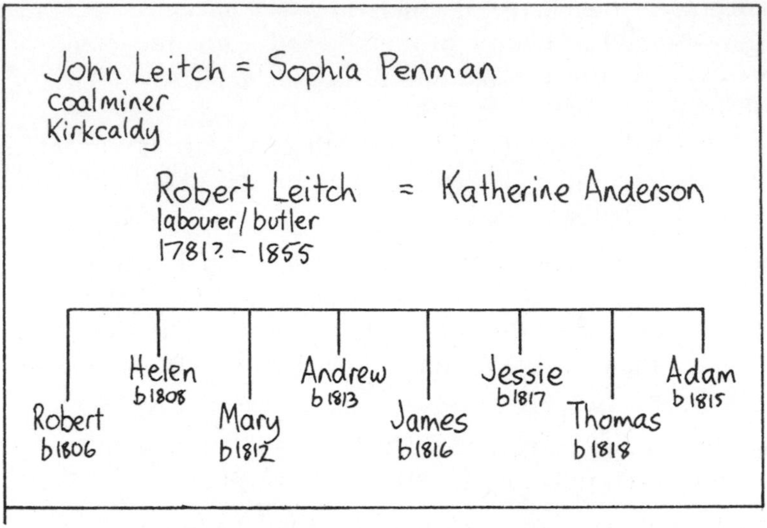

At this stage we have two main alternatives open to us:

1. To go on to the OPRs and try and extend the tree backwards.
2. To consolidate and expand the information on the existing people through census returns and other post-1855 records.

We opt for the census returns to start off with and go up to the library to try and get a seat for a couple of days.

The Census returns

With Robert and his family clearly settled in the Water of Leith for some time, the census returns for that village for 1851 seem a good place to start to see if we can pick up any information.

The Water of Leith comes under Edinburgh so we are able to make use of the street/district index for 1851 to help narrow down the search. Usual procedures—requisition slip indicating CEN 1851 and the books—bring us the enumerator's returns.

Book 25 Entry 37 (we took a long time finding that as there

were no house numbers or even streets in the village) shows:

> Mary Leitch, Head, W, aged 32, provision merchant, born Edinburgh St Cuthberts.
> Catherine Leitch, mother, 64, also b. St Cuthberts.
> Robert Leitch, father, 63, gentleman's servant, b. Kirkcaldy.
> Jamima Healy, daughter, 6, Scholar, b. St Cuthberts.

This provides us with a fine cameo of the family group. Robert and Catherine are living with their daughter, Mary, and 6-year-old granddaughter, Jamima. But Mary is a widow (the letter W) although she is entered under her maiden name of Leitch and not her married name of Healy; and the fact that she is down as a provision merchant suggests that she is carrying on her husband's business. (Water of Leith, as we see from the other returns in the census, was very much a centre for flour and meal milling alongside the fast-flowing stream and close to the big population centre of Edinburgh). There is no doubt that this is our Robert, but once again we have the gentleman's servant description (Water of Leith was very handy indeed for the big houses of the New Town's West End), which confirms our first record of him but does not correspond with his death certificate information.

We also see for our later investigations that the rest of the family were all born in St Cuthbert's parish—a fact that will simplify our searches.

We incidentally take a look at the 1841 Census details for the Water of Leith just to see if there is anything of value—this census was bare in the extreme and not usually worth pursuing if you have enough details from elsewhere. Robert is shown as a labourer this time—and they seem to have got his wife and daughter mixed up as far as ages and names are concerned (the census does not include relationships).

Going back to the marriage of his grandson Robert Leitch and Hepburn Woodcock in 1860, we see another opportunity for expanding the family lines as the marriage comes close to the 1861 Census.

We go through the same routine and look for census returns for the two addresses shown for the bride and groom.

14 Bedford Street, Edinburgh 685/1 Entry 25

We are in luck again, for here we find, a year after the marriage, the groom's family still living at the address—and a large family it is, thanks to the fact that Robert was one of the older offspring and a number of his younger sisters were still living with their parents:

Adam Leitch, head, 46, fishmonger
Isabella Leitch, wife, 46
Mary, daughter, unmarried, 18, dressmaker
Jean, daughter, unmarried, 15, dressmaker
Helen, daughter, 9, scholar
Henrietta, daughter, 7, scholar
Catherine, daughter, 3
Mary McRoberts, boarder, 19, servant

All except the servant are shown as born in Edinburgh. Among the other families occupying the building are a cabinetmaker, a woodcarver, a housepainter, a jeweller and a bootmaker.

This allows us to extend the family tree sideways and to pencil in a few tentative birth dates:

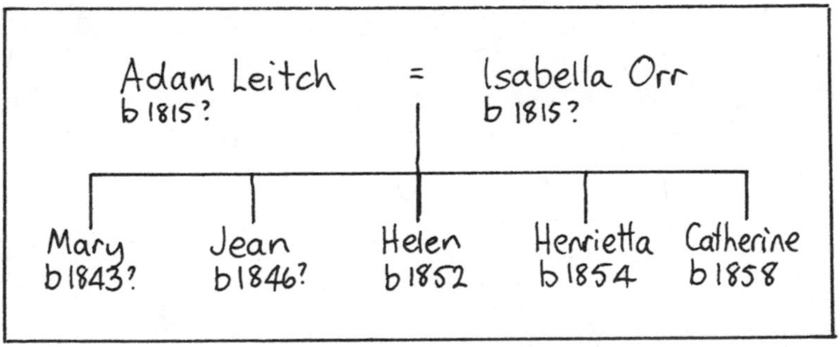

1 Haugh Street, Edinburgh 685/1 Entry 10

When we come to look at the bride's address, from that 1860 marriage we have a little initial difficulty, resulting from the fact that there seems to be no entry for 3 Leggats Land—but do find the family living at 1 Haugh Street, which may be the same place (closes and vennels often carried either their own name or the number of the street which marked their entrance). We may just have been lucky in having the family staying close by the bride's original home. The entry shows that the young couple were sharing their home with the wife's father:

Robert Leitch, head, aged 23, baker, born Edinburgh
Hepburn Leitch, wife, 23, born Forfars Dundee
Hepburn Leitch, daughter, one month, b. Edinburgh
William Woodcock, lodger, widower, 52, upholsterer, b. Dundee
Jamima Woodcock, lodger, 17, b. Edinburgh

This again gives a nice rounded profile of the family: the young couple with new baby, dutifully and traditionally named after the maternal grandmother (and incidentally in this case, the mother), providing a home for the widowed grandfather, William, and for the wife's sister, Jamima. The fact that Hepburn was born in Dundee and her sister (?) Jamima in Edinburgh suggests that the family started in Dundee but between 1838 (birth of older sister) and 1842 (birth of younger sister) moved to Edinburgh. All are items to be noted down for future reference.

The family incidentally seem well housed at 1 Haugh Street, having three rooms which possess one or more windows.

The post-1855 registrations

The original work plus the census returns have given us a large number of people to track down in greater detail in the Births, Marriages and Deaths records. We therefore have a spell down with the indexes again to try and pinpoint some of the events. Among the records we find the following:

Births

- Hepburn Leitch, the little baby mentioned in the 1861

Census returns—and her subsequent brothers, William, Adam, James and Alexander Watt Leitch (the man we started with).

- Catherine Leitch, the three-year-old daughter of Adam Leitch shown in the 1861 Census returns for 14 Bedford Street.

Deaths

We find the death of Isabella Orr, wife of Adam Leitch (1883) and William Woodcock, father of Hepburn Woodcock (1878). This gives us a pair of parents in each case, allowing us to extend Isabella Orr's line thus:

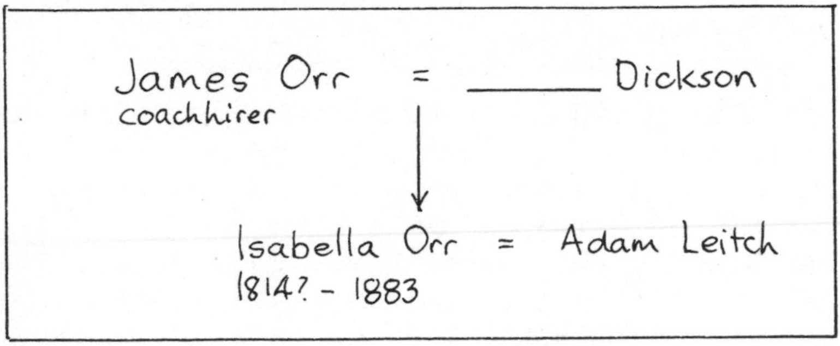

Notice here that the person reporting Isabella's death (her husband Adam) did not know the Christian name of his mother-in-law, although he did know her maiden surname.

William Woodcock, the Dundee upholsterer, has his line extended as follows:

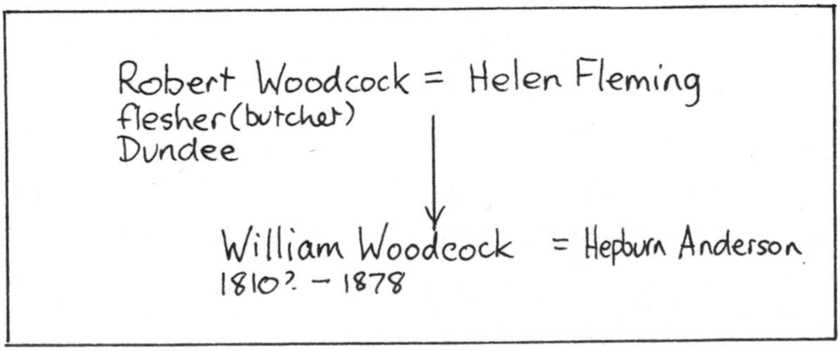

A surprising death we found was that of the Robert Leitch whom we had identified as the father of Alexander Watt Leitch and the groom in the 1860 marriage to Hepburn Woodcock. He died at the very early age of 39, the victim of apoplexy, leaving his wife to cope with four children.

Back to the OPRs

With so much information collected from civil registration and census returns we are well equipped to tackle the daunting field of the Old Parochial Records.

The first target is the background for Robert Leitch, the butler/labourer who moved to Water of Leith after 1800, but who had been born in Kirkcaldy around 1780, the son of John Leitch, coal miner, and Sophia Penman. The two unusual names give us some hope, and we plunge into the OPRs for Kirkcaldy, requisitioning the volume carrying birth entries for that period.

We come up with a good round nothing. Well, almost nothing. We find the odd Leitch (now spelt Leech) and Penman (and even a Sophia or two), but none that tie in firmly with our jig-saw pieces. We try the marriage records, looking for a Leitch marrying a Penman—and find a Penman marrying a Leitch. We find marriage records of a number of what appear to be Robert's brothers—all sons of John Leech, Coal-Grieve at Smitton, but no definite sign of our man. We look at the meagre death records—and come across the death of a John Leech, son of Andrew Leech, coal-hewer, and a victim of the small-pox epidemic which swept the little community in 1773, but, with no clue as to his age even, we cannot assume it is the John Leech we are looking for. Reluctantly, amid all the echoes of the family we are seeking, we call it a day.

Our searches in the OPRs in what is left of our nominal week of searching are confined to the branches other than the main Leitch line. (Even in these days of sex equality, it is the custom to consider the male, name-bearing line as the main one, although genealogy is a hobby in which anything goes,

OPRs are increasingly available on microfilm, but modern technology fails to help Bob Leitch progress beyond ancestor Robert (1780?-1855)

and the person who seeks to find as much as possible about all the families that went into producing him has a load of work on his hands but is adopting a perfectly legitimate stance).

The children of Adam Leitch and Isabella Orr

These children are already clearly listed in our census returns but we are able, through the St Cuthbert's Edinburgh parish records, which are well kept and (glory be!) well indexed in typescript books, to get details of the birth of every one and keep track of the numerous house moves of Adam and Isabella. We trace a few that were not included in the census returns and find that Henrietta was in fact baptised Heneratia (clearly in memory of an uncle—a long run of girls had perhaps led the parents to give up hope of ever producing a male to bear the name!)

The forebears of Katherine Anderson

Having failed with the line of Robert Leitch, 1780?-1855, we try his wife Kathcrine Anderson, knowing that she had been born in St Cuthbert's (census detail). We find her baptismal entry for 1780 and the record of her parents' marriage on 6 July 1760, giving us the names of two of Bob's great-great-great-great-great-grandparents—George Anderson, a miller in the Water of Leith, and William Law, a shoemaker in the same village.

The forebears of Isabella Orr

Similarly, we are in luck with the forebears of Isabella Orr, who married Adam Leitch on 24 March 1837. We are able to find in the well-documented St Cuthbert's parish records her baptismal entry for December 1814, and the marriage record of her parents on 17 July 1798, which gives us the full name of her mother Isabella Dickson (you will remember that her death certificate was lacking on this point)—and for the first time takes the family tree outside Scotland when it was recorded that Isabella Dickson's father was a baker in Liverpool!

The result of all that searching is to provide Bob with an impressive family tree which looks something like the chart on pages 88-9. And that is surely a very substantial platform on which to base any future research into the family history.

Of course, we have only followed the line from one of Bob's grandparents—Alexander Watt Leitch. He has three others to pursue if he's really hooked on the New Register House records!

BASE THREE

The Scottish Record Office

Register House—a tantalising treasure-house of the nation's documentary evidence. If your ancestors are there, how can you track them down?

> Lauritz La Cour and James Boyd should accept of my curious collection of walking sticks one each for their own use, but I wish them to give one each to those of my intimate friends as they may think would prize them.

This sentence comes at the end of a long and rather dreary will made by a Leith businessman and couched in the flat language of his lawyer. Only when he comes to add a sentence to express his thanks in advance to his two friends and executors does his own language show through and we get this delightful glimpse of a character as opposed to a combination of a name, a profession and the dates which bracket a life.

The passage sets the tone for the sort of information which we are likely to find at the next great Base for our ancestor-hunting—Register House, another elegant Georgian edifice, more prominently sited than Base Two, and the home of the Scottish Record Office.

Here the material is enormous, the bulk eclipsing even the store of New Register House and spilling over from the east end of George Street to the new repository, West Register House, at Charlotte Square.

Not only is the bulk of the material so great, its nature is much more unmanageable than those records of Births, Marriages and Deaths that we have been studying. It is essential that we have a very clear picture at this stage of just who our ancestors were, what they did and where they lived. The work we have done at Base Two will help us make the most of what Base Three has to offer.

Once again, the first step is to "sign on"—and in this case it is not going to cost you anything. All you are required to do is make your way to the Historical Search Room and let them know what it is you are after. Family research, the family name and the area should be enough. That information will enable the staff to get some idea of the sort of material you will want to look at—and allow them to give you the right sort of help. You will get a Reader's Ticket, valid until the last day of the calendar year—and you should try and have this with you each time you visit Register House.

The material is, I must repeat, vast in scope and haphazard in nature, but it might help you if I deal with some of the main stores which are of interest to the ancestor-hunter and which are predictable enough to allow for some useful generalisations on what information exists and how to find your way about.

TESTAMENTS AND INVENTORIES

"You can't take it with you, but you can leave it behind" is the basic principle behind wills and testaments—and the importance of making clear just what a dead man's wishes were has handed the legal profession one of its oldest and most cherished tasks: the recording of those wishes.

In Scotland, this act is restricted to the passing on of moveable property (land and buildings come into a different category, as we shall see later), but the documentation relating to it can cover a wealth of information about people and property, family history and financial states. The great accumulation of testaments (including wills where these were made, or testaments dative where the person did not leave express instructions) is for the most part housed in the

Scottish Record Office, indexed (glory be!) and available, for the most part, in good condition and presented in very passable handwriting.

While the basic principle remains the same over the centuries—and indeed much of the language and glimpses into human nature are surprisingly similar—it is worth knowing that there were two main stages as far as the records are concerned. Up until 1822, all testaments were confirmed by the Commissary Courts of Scotland. The origin of these courts lay within the Church and this is reflected in the areas they cover, approximating roughly to the pre-Reformation dioceses—Aberdeen, Argyll, Brechin, Caithness, Dunblane, Dumfries, Dunkeld, Edinburgh, Glasgow, Hamilton & Campsie, Inverness, The Isles, Kirkcudbright, Lanark, Lauder, Moray, Orkney & Shetland, Peebles, Ross, St Andrews, Stirling and Wigtown. These covered the testaments relating to their own area, except for Edinburgh which also exercised an additional overall role, taking in testaments from the length and breadth of Scotland as well as those made by Scots outside their native land.

Fortunately, all testaments are indexed (in volumes according to the relevant Commissary Court, from the earliest recorded examples (ranging from 1514 in Edinburgh to 1700 in Wigtown) up to the year 1800. This work has been done by the Scottish Record Society (and it is unlikely that any of you will get very far in this genealogy game without giving thanks to that fine body!) and gives the Scot and his descendants a distinct advantage over his Sassenach neighbours in this respect.

From 1823 onwards, the Sheriff Courts took over responsibility for confirmation of testaments—and from that date until 1876 there is a little problem in that not all of the sheriff court confirmations are lodged in the Scottish Record Office—some have been kept by the sheriff clerks. From 1876 onwards, an annual list of testaments is issued and that provides a simple means of tracking down the testament you are looking for.

So you want to see if there are any testaments to help you? (They will often be accompanied by inventories of just what was in the house when the person died, usually listed in staggering detail). This is where your work at Base Two begins to pay off. You have the name of a person, the date of his death and the place where he died (although it may be that he made his will elsewhere, so it would be handy to know whether or not he spent his earlier life in some other part of Scotland). These data will enable you to get some idea of just where you should begin your search. Before 1800, as you have seen, the printed indexes make the task more simple. After that date, you may need a little help from the staff in the first instance although you will soon get the hang of it. The filling in of requisition slips here is, thanks to the greater variety of material held, much more complex than the procedure at Base Two.

The information varies considerably with the complexity of the property being willed and the number of bequests and beneficiaries. You can find a wealth of genealogical information or very little, an abundance of personal detail or none at all, a sheaf of insights into the personality of the deceased or no inkling whatsoever. The uncertainty is part of the attraction.

LEGAL AND GENERAL

The other great comprehensive funds of information are the *Registers of Sasines* (many and complex in the early years but gradually simplified until in 1926 they became a single central register). These relate to changes of land ownership while the *Services of Heirs* relate to succession and are well indexed after 1700, providing extracted information which may make it unnecessary to consult the original (often in Latin). *Court cases* are particularly fine sources of insight into the lives of Scots, high and low, so persevere with the rather haphazard wealth of indexes here. Similar effort is needed with the *Deeds*, a wealth of detail on all sorts of subjects under the sun.

BASE FOUR

The Libraries

DICKIE, MATTHEW, M.A. 1876.
Minister of South U.P. Church, Sanquhar.

DICKIE, MATTHEW MURE, M.A. 1870, B.D. 1874.
Sometime U.P. Minister at Haddington; resigned in 1886 owing to ill-health; resident in Bristol, 1896.

DICKIE, ROBERT, M.D. 1842.
"Hibernus" [Grad. Alb.].

DICKIE, ROBERT, M.A. 1887.
Schoolmaster in (1) South Public School, Paisley, (2) Central Public School, Gourock, (3) Kibble Reformatory Institution, Paisley, (4) Hutchesons' Grammar School, Glasgow, (5) Public School, Skelmorlie.

DICKIE, ROBERT PITTENDRIGH, M.A. 1885.
F.C. Minister at Longriggend.

DICKIE, WILLIAM, M.D. 1844, C.M. 1863.
Belize, Honduras.

DICKIE, WILLIAM, M.A. 1875.
U.P. Minister at (1) Rosehearty, (2) Perth, (3) Dowanhill, Glasgow.

DICKINSON, JOHN, M.A. 1883, B.Sc. 1886, M.B., C.M. 1887.
Campbeltown; Kirkdale, Liverpool; died at Kintillo, Bridge of Earn, 13th September, 1890.

DICKSON, ALEXANDER, LL.D. 1879.
M.D. Edin. 1860; Professor of Botany in (1) The School of Physic in Ireland, 1866 to 1868, (2) Glasgow University, 1868 to 1879, (3) Edinburgh University, 1879 to 1887; born in Edinburgh, 21st February, 1836; died suddenly, of heart disease, on 30th December, 1887, during the interval of a curling match at Thriepland Pond, near Hartree, his residence in Peeblesshire.

DICKSON, ALEXANDER, M.B., C.M. 1883.
Ship Surgeon; Baillieston; Yeovil, Somerset.

DICKSON, CHARLES SCOTT, M.A. 1871.
(1) Writer, Glasgow; (2) Advocate, Edinburgh; Lecturer on Constitutional Law and History in Glasgow University during Summer 1878; Solicitor-General for Scotland, 1896; Q.C. 1896; brother of James Douglas Hamilton Dickson, M.A. (q.v.).

DICKSON, DAVID, D.D. 1824.
Minister of (1) High Church, Kilmarnock, (2) St. Cuthbert's, Edinburgh; died 28th July, 1842, aged 63; officiated at funeral of Sir Walter Scott.

DICKSON, GEORGE, M.D. 1839.
"Hibernus" [Grad. Alb.].

DICKSON, GEORGE, M.B., C.M. 1881, M.D. 1885.
Glasgow; son of Professor William Purdie Dickson (q.v.).

If you are not used to them, Reference Libraries can be offputting. Persevere—and the rewards could be enormous

ONE PERSON I was attempting to track down disappeared mysteriously from the Scottish records and re-appeared again many years later, with no hint as to how the intervening years had been spent. The clue came in a list of Edinburgh medical graduates which revealed that the thesis for which he had been awarded his MD was on the subject of the body structure of the alligator. With these creatures, to put it mildly, thin on the ground in Morningside, this was, as it turned out, a pointer to missing years spent across the seas.

This little gem is typical of the kind of totally indefinable information which is carried in the reference libraries, the specialist libraries and the local libraries of Scotland, providing an insight sometimes into the genealogical details of a family but more often into the actual life of individuals.

Many people have been used to wandering along the fiction areas of libraries, with books grouped tidily by author, and all the Agatha Christies side by side, or along open reference shelves with all the goodies on display—the dictionaries of quotations, the atlases and the guides to butterflies of Great Britain. To such readers, the mysteries of the large reference libraries, where the shelves represent just the tip of the iceberg, may seem unfathomable.

Getting to grips with this type of reference library can pay very large dividends for the ancestor-hunter and it is worth the effort to achieve that familiarity. Two factors operate in favour of the newcomer.

Firstly, the librarians themselves. In these days of changing attitudes to service and the public, librarians along with postmen have mercifully retained the old-fashioned virtues of caring and cheerfulness. So if you can pick a time when they are not too busy, make yourself known to the librarians—explain your unfamiliarity with the system and spell out just what it is you are hoping to find, even if that gives away an understandable vagueness at this stage.

Secondly, there are the indexes, the heart of any reference library. Browse through them, get to know them. Note any fascinating section which you feel may be of interest.

What you are searching for will not be a straightforward item such as those we have been speaking about at the other Base Points. Now it will be very dependent on the facts which you have unearthed at those earlier stages. You may not even know that the information which relates to you exists, let alone where it is in the library. Serendipity—the art of making fortunate discoveries—is now a major partner in your efforts. But you must give it a chance to operate by exposing it to all the possible areas where luck can play a part.

It is difficult for me to tell anyone what to look for at this stage, but here are just a few random thoughts, with illustrations, to whet your appetite and keep you browsing at the Reference shelves and indexes.

1. Trade directories

Started for the larger urban centres in the second half of the eighteenth century, trade directories at first were concerned very much with the gentry and the professional men. Rapidly they came to be service guides, very much the Georgian Yellow Pages of Scotland, where you could find a pastrycook or a cowfeeder, a surgeon or an artificial leg-maker. Selections of these directories will be available at the big reference libraries (and indeed at the libraries you have already been using at New Register House and Register House), but the really fine runs will be held in the relevant area library—for example the Edinburgh Room at Edinburgh Central Library will be the place to go if you are looking for a continuous set of Edinburgh & Leith street directories, the Mitchell library if you are focussed on Glasgow.

The information carried in these directories is enormous. They usually list people alphabetically, by street and by occupation. Bear in mind the following points:

- The directories are trade publications—they may therefore throw more light on what your forebears did than the civil registration did. One of my wife's ancestors was described in some 14 entries in the statutory registers (births, marriages and deaths of his children) as a copper engraver. Only in the street directories did we find that, although he was indeed a copper engraver, he was in fact a specialist engraver of sheet music.

  The later street directories even give a person's employer in many instances. An insurance clerk may have the information "Sun Fire" added in brackets, the printer may have his publication added.

- Trade directories may often give a person's trading address *and* his home address. This can provide a useful guide to, for example, the extent or growth of a person's business. I followed the progress of a pharmacist from one shop (1865 directory) to five shops (1876 directory) in this way.

- Trade directories go much lower down the scale than even census returns do—and in particular often give the jobs of women—where these are not specified in either census or registration returns. A person who was never more than a mother-and-wife statistic in the OPRs appeared as a sick-nurse in the street directory.

- Trade directories often go well beyond the boundaries of the city to take in small townships on the outskirts and country gentry. Check this.
- Directories usually carried additional advertising—take a look at these announcements, especially if the person you are tracking was in the type of self-employed business that needed promotion.
- Directories carried a great deal of additional information on, say, delivery charges within the city. Take a look at these pages.

2. Lists of graduates and students

Universities and schools have published useful directories which provide information that often goes much further than one would expect. I picked at random (promise!) two such directories, for Glasgow University and for Aberdeen Grammar School, and opened at random (again, I promise!) to show the variety of information that is carried and, I hoped, the potential gems which lurked in such columns.

The Glasgow University lists gave ample examples of the extremes that you are likely to encounter.

As you see from page 112, if you were unlucky enough to be searching for Robert Dickie (number 3 on the page) you would be disappointed to come away with only the information that he was Hibernus (Grad A1b) and MD1842—guaranteed to send you scurrying to the introduction of the book to find out just what that meant.

If, however, you were after Alexander Dickson (middle of the page) what a wealth of information is at your finger tips—including the information that he died suddenly of heart disease during the interval of a curling match at Thriepland Pond! I bet that wasn't all carried on his death certificate.

And if you were on the trail of David Dickson (three places down), what a real gem to come away with—he officiated at the funeral of Sir Walter Scott.

***DANIELSON, James Gordon.** **1896-1901**
[S. of Rev. Andrew D., D.D.], Chindwara, India. b. 15 February 1888. Entd. Lower I.

In service of Bank of Scotland, 1904-08; passed membership examination of the Institute of Bankers, Edinburgh, 1908; in service of Hongkong and Shanghai Banking Corporation in London, 1908-10; in Hamburg, 1910-11; in New York, 1911-15; in Yokohama, Japan, from December 1919.

2nd Lieut., 1st Highland Brigade, R.F.A. (T.F.), 6 Oct. 1915. Served in France and Belgium with the 51st Highland Div., 1916; and with the Lahore Div., Sept. 1916 to 1918. Acting Lieut., Nov. 1916; Lieut., Aug. 1917. Discharged 2 May 1919.

DANSON, Arthur Llewellyn. **1885-1889**
S. of Rev. J. M. D., 18 King Street. Age 10. Entd. Classical I.

B.A. Oxon., 1898; passed into Indian Civil Service, 1898; served in the Punjab as assistant commissioner; under-secretary to Government, 1905-07; registrar, Chief Court, Punjab, 1908; died at Lahore, as result of an accident, 27 March 1912.

DANSON, Edmund Wilmot. **1887-1892**
S. of Rev. J. Myers D., 18 King Street. Age 9. Entd. Middle I.

Served sea apprenticeship in Aberdeen White Star Line; attached to Royal Navy (Channel Squadron), 1897-98; joined Royal Indian Marine, 1899; engaged mostly on survey of coast of Persian Gulf and South India; took part in Somali Expedition (medal); died at Moulmein, Burma, as result of a shooting accident, 23 May 1921.

Naval Transport Officer, Bombay (lent from Royal Indian Marine). Commander, R.I.M., Jan. 1917.

DANSON, E[rnest] D[enny] Logie. **1892-1894**
S. of Rev. [J. Myers] D., Ingleboro' House, Castlehill. Age 12. Entd. Classical I.

M.A., 1902; tutor in York, 1902-04; student, Episcopal Theological College, Edinburgh, 1904-1906; ordained deacon, 1906; priest, 1907; assistant curate, S. Paul's Cathedral, Dundee, 1906-11; S. Andrew's Cathedral, Singapore, 1911-1912; acting chaplain in Java, 1913; chaplain of Seremban, F.M.S., 1914; bishop of Labuan and Sarawak, 1917. D.D. Aberd., 1921.

Chaplain and Hon. Captain, Malay States Volunteer Rifles, 1 Jan. 1916. Resigned commission on appointment to Bishopric of Labuan and Sarawak.

DANSON, James Gordon. **1894-1903**
S. of Rev. J. Myers D., Ingleboro' House, Castlehill. b. 1 March 1885. Entd. Middle I.

M.B., Ch.B., 1908; M.D., 1922; surgeon, Royal Navy, 1910.

Served with Mediterranean Fleet, 1914; with Grand Fleet, 1915; in South Irish Waters (Queenstown), 1915; Egypt, 1916-17; at R.N. Barracks, Chatham, 1918. Surgeon Lieutenant-Commander, 1918 (ante-dated to 1916).

***DANSON, John Rhys.** **1897-1903**
S. of Rev. James [Myers] D., 19 Bon-Accord Crescent. b. 24 July 1887. Entd. Middle I.

Served apprenticeship as mechanical engineer with Messrs. Clyne, Mitchell & Company, Aberdeen; assistant engineer, Dundee Corporation Electricity Supply Department, 1908; second engineer in the power station, La Plata, Buenos Aires, 1914; assistant municipal electrical engineer, Georgetown, Penang, S.S., 1919.

Private, 14th Batt. London Regiment (London Scottish) (T.F.), 17 Dec. 1914. Served in France, June to Nov. 1916; in Salonika to June 1917; in Palestine to June 1918; in Belgium to Feb. 1919. Sergt., 20 Dec. 1914; Company Sergt. Major, 4 June 1915; Regmtl. Sergt. Major, 22 Nov. 1916. Mentioned, 29 March and 25 Oct. 1917. D.C.M., 21 Aug. 1918. Demobd. 5 March 1919.

DAVIDSON, Alexander. **1869-1870**
[S. of Alexander D.], Tarves. Age 17. Entd. II.

Farmer, Cairnhill and Little Meldrum, Tarves.

***DAVIDSON, Alexander.** **1881-1886**
S. of Alexander D., Mains of Cairnbrogie, Tarves. Age 12. Entd. Middle II.

Entered service of the Northern Assurance Company, Aberdeen, as junior clerk, 1889; now cashier.

DAVIDSON, Alexander. **1884-1887**
S. of Rev. George D., Logie Coldstone, Dinnet. Age 14. Entd. Classical II.

Served apprenticeship with Messrs. Walker and Beattie, land surveyors, Aberdeen; in 1892 went to South Africa, subsequently becoming manager of the New Kleinfontein Gold Mining Company, Benoni; served as a volunteer throughout the South African War, receiving the Queen's Medal with four clasps; died at Kleinfontein Farm, Benoni, 9 January 1915.

***DAVIDSON, Alexander Aitken.** **1900-[1907]**
S. of Thomas D., 13 Affleck Street. b. 3 April 1891. Entd. Lower II.

Of Messrs. Davidsons (Aberdeen), Limited, wholesale fish merchants, Aberdeen.

Private, 4th Batt. Gordon Highlanders (T.F.), Oct. 1914. Promoted Sergeant. 2nd Lieut., 4th Batt. Gordon Highlanders, Nov. 1914. Served at home. Demobd. on medical grounds, 1917 (Lieut.).

***DAVIDSON, Alexander Campbell.** **1904-1906**
S. of Alexander D., Broomhill Park. b. 26 April 1896. Entd. Lower III.

1681 WILLIAM CARNEGIE, M.A.; trans. from Careston in 1681; trans. to Arbroath after 3rd June 1686.

1686 ALEXANDER GUTHRIE, M.A. (Edinburgh 1682); pres. by William, Duke of Queensberry, and Robert, Earl of Southesk, 24th and 27th May, coll. 26th Oct., and inst. 7th Dec. 1686; dep. by Presb. of Dumfries 16th June 1691, "for profaning the sacrament of baptism," etc. —[*G. R. Hornings*, 7th July 1688; *MS. Acc. of Min.*, 1689; *Dumfries Presb. Reg.*]

1696 ANDREW DARLING, M.A.; ord. before 13th Oct. 1696; trans. to Kinnoull between 11th May and 26th Dec. 1697.

1700 JAMES CURRIE, M.A. (Edinburgh, 13th July 1695); licen. by Presb. of Earlston 16th Sept. 1697; called by Presb. *jure devoluto*, and ord. 9th May 1700; died 25th Feb. 1726, aged 52. He marr. Isobel Bell, who survived him, and had issue—James, min. of Middlebie; John; Andrew; Helen (marr. Thomas Bell, in Westside of Blacksyke); Agnes; Janet; Sybella.—[*Tombst.*]

1729 ALEXANDER ORR, born 1686, son of Alexander O., min. of St Quivox; licen. by Presb. of Ayr 22nd June 1715; ord. to Muirkirk 5th June 1717; called 26th Feb., trans. and adm. 10th July 1729; died 19th June 1767. He marr. 25th Jan. 1722, Agnes (died 21st May 1760), daugh. of John Dalrymple of Waterside, and had issue—Agnes, born 9th Nov. 1722 (marr. William Young, min. of Hutton); Barbara, born 10th Oct. 1723 (marr. John Craig, min. of Ruthwell); Alexander, W.S., born 23rd March 1725, died 27th Nov. 1774; Peter, born 12th Oct. 1727; John, merchant, Virginia; Susan (marr. 1768, William Murray, second son of William M. of Murraythwaite).—[*Tombst.*; M'Call's *Some Old Families.*]

1768 ALEXANDER BROWN, trans. from Tongland, and adm. 26th July 1768; trans. to Moffat 30th Oct. 1783.

1784 JAMES YORSTOUN, born 17th Dec. 1755, son of Peter Y., min. of Closeburn; licen. by Presb. of Penpont 5th July 1775; ord. to Middlebie 23rd March 1778; pres. by William, Duke of Queensberry 8th Jan., and adm. 1st July 1784; died 6th April 1834. He marr. 2nd Oct. 1817, Margaret (died 25th March 1828), daugh. of James Currie Carlyle of Brydekirk. Publication—Account of the Parish (Sinclair's *Stat. Acc.*, iii., xxi.).

1834 ROBERT MENZIES, born 31st Jan. 1801, son of William M., min. of Lanark; educated at the Grammar School there, High School, Edinburgh (dux 1816), and Univ. of Edinburgh; licen. by Presb. of Lanark 4th Aug. 1824; pres. by Lieut.-General Matthew Sharpe of Hoddam, and ord. 2nd Sept. 1834; D.D. (Edinburgh, April 1864); died 6th July 1877. He marr. 28th Oct. 1835, Martha Reid (died 19th July 1875), daugh. of Robert Coldstream, merchant, Leith, and Elizabeth, daugh. of John Phillips, and had issue—William, min. of Duns; Robert Coldstream, born 11th July 1839, died 1st Sept. 1870; Allan, born 23rd June 1841, died 29th Nov. 1892; John Coldstream, lieut. R.E., born 8th April 1843, died 2nd May 1866; Elizabeth Phillips, born 23rd June 1844, died 29th July 1865; Jeanie Newbigging, born 23rd Sept. 1845, died at Hyeres, France, 8th March 1892; Martha Reid Coldstream, born 12th April 1847, died 18th May 1914; Lawrie, engineer, born 16th June 1848, died at Alexandrowsk, South Russia, 11th Dec. 1914; Francis, born 22nd June, died 16th Dec. 1849; Alexander Charles, born 23rd Aug. 1850, died 24th March 1875; Catherine Cowan, born 13th Oct. 1852, died 18th Oct. 1879. Publications—*Exposition of St Paul's Epistle to the Romans* (trans. from the German of F. A. Tholuck), 2 vols. (Edinburgh, 1833-6); *Exposition, Doctrinal and Philological, of Christ's Sermon on the Mount* (trans. from the German of F. A. Tholuck), 2 vols. (Edinburgh, 1834-7); *Answers to Robert Haldane's Strictures on Tholuck's Epistle to the Romans* (Edinburgh, 1838); *Cuff, the Negro Boy* (trans.

Obviously what went into those directories depended entirely on the information provided by the individuals (indeed I felt so guilty that I for once filled in the form I get annually from my own college and let them know just what I had been doing over the years).

The Aberdeen Grammar School lists makes much the same point. If you were looking for Alexander Davidson (second column, name two) you would gain little that would not arise from the Births, Marriages and Deaths. But if you were looking into the Danson family you would find five brothers on that same page. They seem moreover to provide the archetypal pattern for the great age of the international Scot—one a civil servant in the Punjab, one a bishop in Labuan, one a surgeon in the Royal Navy, one an engineer working from Buenos Aires to Penang, one a naval man and explorer.

Take a look at the other entries and get some feel of the potential of such a publication to anyone involved in not just tracing ancestors but learning something about their lives.

3. The Ministers of Scotland

If you are very lucky, one of your ancestors will have been a minister in the Church of Scotland. Of all the professions, this is one which is arguably the best documented from the genealogist's point of view. The great *Fasti Ecclesiae Scotiae* details in many volumes the ministers ordained by the Church over the centuries. The entries seek to provide as much information as possible not only on the man's service within the Church but also on his family. Take a look at the page opposite, again selected at random. It relates to the south-west of Scotland (the early volumes are divided up according to the synod in which the minister worked) and refers to the parishes in Annan Synod of Hoddam, Ecclefechan and Luce.

Again, the amount of information varies mightily, but just ponder on some of those entries. Pick out the enormous amount of genealogical information—one could build up a fine family tree solely on the basis of that information. And consider the wealth of detail which would help solve what

Hector's) spouse has compeired before the congregation three severall times but was not yet absolved and he had caused advertise her to attend this diet. And being called she compeired and her sin with its aggravations being set home on her conscience and she seeming serious and penitent was removed. The Session being satisfied with her appointed she might compeir once more before the congregation and be absolved, and she being called in the same was intimate to her.

Alexander Gray and Janet Spence have satisfied discipline and are absolved. **Alexander Gray and Janet Spence absolvd.**

Session clos'd with prayer.

SESSION HELD AT ROTHESAY JUNE 29TH, 1720.

After prayer.

Sederunt: Master Dugald Stewart, minister; James Stewart, provost, Thomas Wallace, bailiff; Robert Wallace, late bailiff; James, Edward and John Stewarts; Alexander and Donald Leeches; Robert Glass and John M'Conachy, elders; and John Gealy, Donald Nivin, Donald Bannatyne and William M'Gilcherran, deacons.

The severall ordinary collections since last accompt with the treasurer, November 4th, 1719, amount to 60 lib. 2s. 4d. which with 11s. 4d. that remaind in his hands comes to 60 lib. 13s. 8d. whereof given to severall indigent persons and approven by the Session 15l. 12s. There remains 45l. 1s. 8d. whereof the Session appoints to be distribute in manner following, vizt. one pound four shillings Scots each to Helen Stewart, John Morison, Margaret Glass, Jeals N'Thomas, Janet Spence, Margaret Stewart, and Cathrine N'Arthur; and one lib. each to John M'Kinlay's orphans, Janet Gealy, Elspeth Black, Donald M'Neil, Gilbert M'Kinlay, Bryce Frazer, Elspeth Wallace, and Ninian Stewart; and sixteen shillings Scots each to Blind John M'Gilcherran, Walter M'Alaster, Cathrine N'Conachy, Cathrine N'Alaster, Janet Beith, Isobel N'Curdy, Jane N'Gilcherran, and Isobel N'Neil; and thirteen shillings four pennies each to Mary N'Gilchattan, Donald M'Eachan, Mary Stewart, Mary Heman, James M'Tyre, Christian Nivin, Janet N'Gilcherran, Elspeth Frazer and Christian Campbell; *item* half a crown to help the payment of one Seymore's cure, and one pound two shillings four pennies for new cloaths to Isobel N'Curdy (her old ones having been stollen), in all now distribute 31l. 8s. 4d., which taken from the abovesaid 45l. 1s. 8d. the treasurer remains debitor to the Session in 13l. 13s. 4d. **Collections and distribution of charity.**

could be problem areas—it tells us that Alexander Orr's son John went off to be a merchant in Virginia, that Robert Menzies' son Lawrie drowned at Alexandrowsk, South Russia.

4. Session Books

Keeping with the Church, it is worth mentioning that in some areas the Session Books, mainly referring to the earlier period before 1855 civil registration (and sometimes the basis for those OPRs you have been studying at Base Two), have been printed by local interests—and offer a much easier way of delving into the doings of your eighteenth-century ancestors. This is where the librarian will come in handy, knowing from your information which areas you are interested in. The local libraries are understandably the most likely source of this type of publicaion. The page opposite comes from the Session Book of Rothesay and covers a large number of names in what must have been a fairly small community. If you can find a similar publication for the parish in which your forebears lived you may very well find them mentioned in the pages, either as the elders dispensing moral judgments, or as parishioners at the receiving end of charity (in our extract you will see that Isobel N'Curdy received "one pound two shillings four pennies for new cloaths—her old ones having been stollen"), or punishment (the pages are packed with moral pronouncements on backsliding among the faithful, generally as regards sexual relations!).

5. Scotland under the minister's eye

Perhaps the finest work to come from a Church source was the massive *Statistical Account*, the brainchild of Sir John Sinclair. In the late 1700s, anxious to produce a definitive study of Scotland (he was an agriculturist, businessman and imaginative thinker), he asked every parish minister in Scotland to produce a survey of his parish (Sinclair produced guidelines as to what they should look for)—and the result of this enormous undertaking is to be found in most large reference libraries in Scotland. (The success of Sinclair's venture can be judged by the fact that subsequent Statistical Accounts have been carried out from time to time, using a very similar basis for their scope and treatment).

By this stage, you will certainly have identified the parish in which your ancestors lived. You will also, if things have gone with even average smoothness, have got back to the sort of period (1790s) when this first Statistical Account was being prepared. You are now offered a thumbnail sketch (sometimes quite a hefty thumbnail) of exactly what was happening in that very parish. How much were the labourers paid? What equipment was used on the farms? What crops were grown? What factories existed? You will even find that the minister (and incidentally the quality of the reporting varies considerably with the ability and dedication of individual clergymen) was even asked to list the worthies and famous men born in the parish. Values change, and the famous men listed in 1790 are not necessarily the ones who are known now. You may even find that someone whom you considered an unknown ancestor was in fact a famous ancestor. We did when we came to look up the parish of Cramond and found that my wife's grandfather had not been the first to go to Ireland from Scotland—his great-great-great-grandmother's brother had made the trip nearly 200 years earlier and set up the School of Anatomy in Dublin!

These then are some tit-bits to set the intellectual gastric juices flowing. Get along to the nearest reference library and see what it has to offer. You will be surprised.

BASE FIVE

On Location

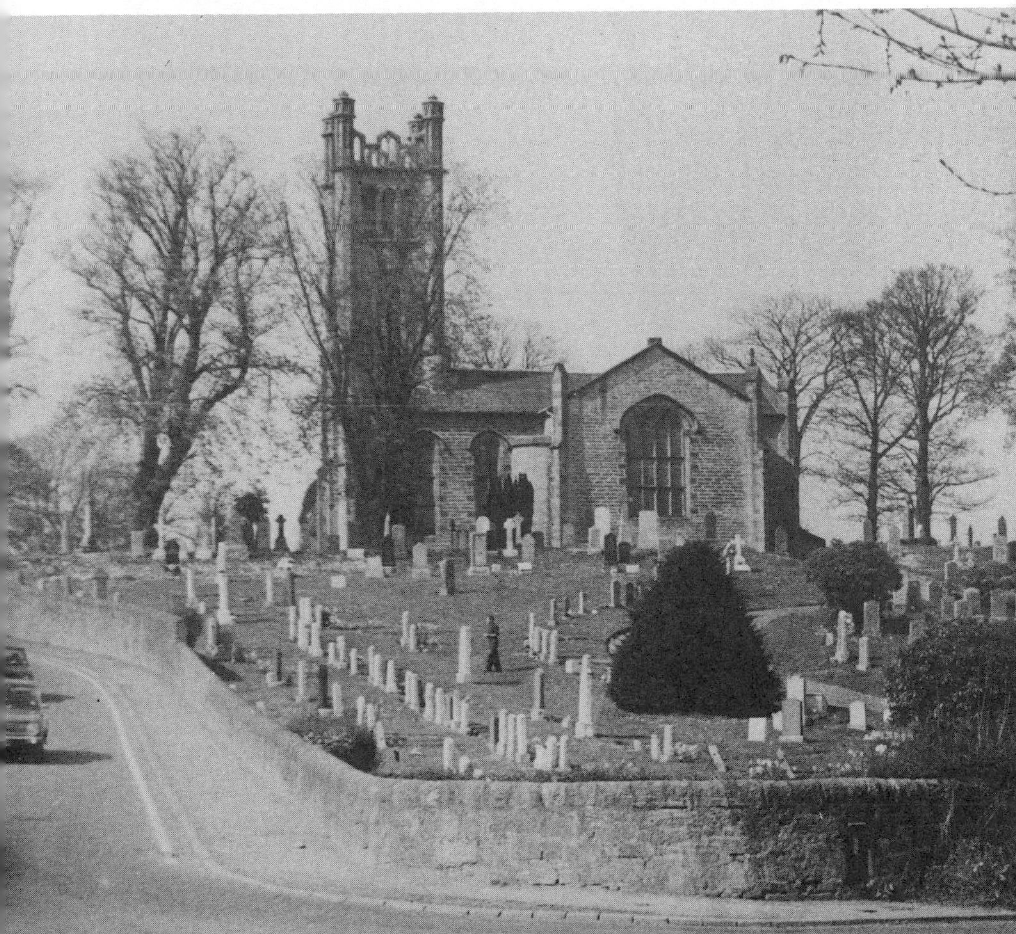

A visit to the places where your ancestors lived and worked can have a lot to offer the genealogist

THE PHOTOGRAPH illustrating Base Five shows my twin sons, Steve and Kevin, in Carrubbers Close, a narrow alleyway opening off Edinburgh's Royal Mile, just south of the Old Tron Kirk.

Steve and Kevin were born in 1966. Their great-great-great-great-grandmother, Anne Dundas, was born two hundred years earlier in 1766. Carrubbers Close was the narrow access to the congested housing where Anne and her husband, shoemaker James Balbirnie, lived out the last few decades of their lives—both of them passing their eightieth birthday. Anne worked as a sicknurse and it was from this Close that she operated during the cholera epidemic of 1832 which swept along the High Street, killing 600 people in six months, including some from the buildings where Anne and James lived.

A visit to an actual location such as this—and you are not always lucky enough to find the location even remotely reminiscent of the conditions of 150 years ago—can do a lot not perhaps to add to your totting up of ancestral names but certainly to your understanding of the conditions in which your ancestors lived and worked. The Close has, believe it or not, been considerably widened since the days when it contributed to housing, between North Bridge and the Netherbow, the most congested habitations in Europe. Nevertheless, a visit can do more than a book or an engraving to take you back to those days and those settings.

With more and more of your ancestors emerging and coming to life, it is only natural that you too will want to see the places in which all those Births, Marriages and Deaths were taking place. Some of you may be lucky enough to live close at hand; for others it will mean a trip of some distance and even call for a lengthy outlay for travel and board. Is it worth it? What can you possibly get out of a visit that couldn't be collected more conveniently from books and records?

The answers to those questions will vary considerably with individual cases and may even depend on your own powers of imagination! You don't have to be Thomas Gray in the churchyard at Stoke Poges or Oliver Goldsmith confronted by the Deserted Village to find that stones and structures, scenes and settings, can tell you as much as books and records about the life of your forebears.

You will by this stage have acquired a wealth of detail as far as addresses and occupations are concerned. If these are centred mainly in rural areas, that old Ordnance Survey map which I advised in Base One will now come into its own, while if your targets are more in Scotland's towns and cities, you will need an up-to-date street map.

Homes and houses

The chances of finding the actual houses in which your family lived a century ago will again vary from one case to the next, but one fortunate by-product of Scotland's poor housing record and high proportion of old housing stock is the existence, in varying degrees of maintenance, of a higher proportion of old houses than you will find in some of the more opulent and favoured areas of the United Kingdom.

It is worth emphasising that the sooner you start, the better chance you have of finding the houses. I came to Scotland in 1970 and took a few years before we got down to the business of tracking down my wife's Scottish ancestors. Key addresses for the 1840-60 period lay in the old Dumbiedykes area of Edinburgh. I arrived, complete with camera, to find that the two addresses which figured on our family tree had been demolished only a year previously—and there was a bulldozer actually at work on the block where an army-pensioner great-great-uncle was a janitor in 1881.

Let's imagine that you are very lucky and some of the homes are still standing. They will almost certainly have been updated and restructured to some extent, but they will still be worth a photograph—not just of the house itself, but also of the street and any features (a church, a factory), which might have survived from the time your ancestors lived there. I have always found it diplomatic to ask permission of any people living in the house at the present time. After all, just imagine looking out of the window of your own lounge and seeing someone clicking away at your frontage. The courteous act may even bring in a few bonuses about number of rooms, when the extensions were made, etc.

Photographs

A slight digression on the subject of photographs. The material you are assembling is not just for yourself and not just for the present moment. It is therefore advisable to take the advice:

PLEASE AVOID
POLAROID

The provision of photographic prints on tap is undoubtedly valuable in certain instances, but if you are putting together a portfolio of illustrations of houses and settings, you are concerned not with immediate delivery, but with two elements—quality and ease of reproduction—which are not the strongpoints of Polaroid cameras. Be patient, aim for good colour or black-and-white negatives and you have a source of photographs which will do full justice to the work you have put into the rest of the subject—and which can be reproduced for other members of the family.

Back to the business in hand. You may of course not be lucky enough to find intact and charming the cottage where your great-great-grandparents lived or the mill where the man of the house toiled. But, as we have seen, there are other subjects to be photographed. You may not be able to photograph the cottage, but what about the view from the front door? The street in which the house existed? The church? The river? The bridge? There are a hundred-and-one elements which played a part in the life of that family, some of which may still be standing there waiting to be photographed.

There are two buildings which call for particular attention, the church and the local library. By the very nature of your records, the church will have played a central part in the baptisms, weddings and funerals which provided the basis for so much of the work done at Base Two. Churches have been more carefully conserved than ordinary dwelling houses. It is much more likely that you will find the church where a couple were married in 1850, 1800 or even 1750 than the building where they set up house. So visit the church—get your photographs taken—the porch where the couple stood after the wedding, the font which came a little later, and do not of course neglect that greatest of assets to the genealogist, the graveyards.

There is, paradoxically, something living about a gravestone which means so much more than the bare record of an interment. The task calls for plodding and patience and good waterproof shoes. But persevere—and don't just look for your own family's gravestones. You'll be astonished at just what you can pick up from the others, especially in the small rural areas where the farming families were compact and interlinked. I once went to photograph my grandfather's gravestone, got lost and found *his* father's—a stone whose existence had not been known to any of his present descendants.

If you are fortunate enough to find gravestones, take care

Even in a developed city, a location visit is worthwhile. Colinton still allows the visitor to make out some of the features of the old village (*above*), while Bob Leitch found the Dean Village (*below*) very similar to the setting in which his ancestors lived in the 1700s

with the photography. A little brush would not come amiss and, more effective still, try and choose your moment when a low and slanting sun makes the most of any faded lettering. I have also seen effective rubbings taken of gravestones using soft white paper and black-heelball in the same way as brass rubbings are made.

The local library is one source of valuable information which is quite easy to overlook. It is unlikely that it will be bristling with volumes to the same extent as the large central reference libraries we have mentioned in Base Four, but it will make up for any disadvantage in size in its specialisation in the area you are interested in. This will not just manifest itself in the obvious way with such items as files of local newspapers. It may also be reflected in small publications or essays by, say, the local history club. The small local library will also be able to tip you off on any exhibitions or museums in the area which are worth visiting.

BASE SIX

The Museums of Scotland

Step back into your Highland past at Kingussie Folk Museum—complete with whale vertebra stools at the door

Scotland's new folk museums—time machines that can take you back into the lives of your ancestors

WHEN WE moved into a house in Gorebridge in 1976, we came across a strange object in the garden. Heavy enough to pose problems to a small child, weird in shape, puzzling in consistency, it appeared to be vegetable or possibly animal, but certainly not mineral. The weathering had had an effect and its surface was losing a former smoothness. A knowing and visiting friend put us right. "It's the vertebra of a large whale." And that was that. Why anyone would want a spinal cotton-reel, no matter how imposing, did not seem a worthwhile question to ask, but a year later we got the answer. Visiting the delightful folk museum in Lewis which owed its origin to the enthusiastic school children of Shawbost, we saw not one but two of our vertebrae! And a placard told us just what they were used for—not as some early Barbara Hepworth to decorate a whaler's cottage (there was no room for such frivolity as that) but for the more mundane function of providing stools for the young children!

The simple and perhaps insignificant fact emerged from one of Scotland's new wave of folk museums which can take you back, in a way very few books or films can, into the lives of your ancestors. By now you will have traced quite a number of forebears and will quite naturally have wanted to progress from knowing when they lived and who they married, how many children they had and what they died of, to wanting to try and share in their existence, to know something of the style and quality of their life rather than its duration, about the places in which the family lived and worked, ate and slept.

The museums which concentrate on social history have developed naturally as our attitudes to history itself have changed. We are now no longer satisfied with tales of treaties and triumphs, dynasties and politics. As a result, there are now throughout Scotland a number of specialised museums where you can turn back the centuries and pitch yourself into the lives of your ancestors, whether they lived (or worked) in a grand house in Edinburgh's New Town, a Black House in the far north, a fishing cottage in Fife or a miner's cottage in Dalkeith. The fisherman and the farmer, the cobbler and the miner, the weaver and the fireman, the fishmonger and the carter—all are catered for in Scotland's developing network of "Roots" museums.

ANCESTORS AT HOME

The domestic lives of our forebears are well presented in a number of first-class Scottish museums. Here is a selection:

1. A Georgian Townhouse

In the finest of Adam town square of all, Edinburgh's Charlotte Square, a superbly refurbished house has rapidly established itself among the city's top tourist attractions. From the elegant drawing-room to the fascinating kitchen, the whole building is decked out in the style of 1800—even down to removing many of the Victorian "improvements." And even if your ancestors did not aspire to style such as this, remember just how many Scots worked as domestic servants. This house is as relevant to them as it is to the owners. While it is typically Edinburgh, it does at the same time represent a standard which the gentry in a number of Scottish towns from Perth to Dumbarton, from Peebles to Nairn, would be attempting to emulate—and as such will provide as much of an insight into their lives as to those of the capital's aristocracy.

2. Earlier Townhouse

Across the valley, brooding on the rocky ridge from the Castle to the Palace, lies the Old Town of Edinburgh and it too has acquired a fine and worthy counterpart to the Georgian House in the beautifully transformed Gladstones Land, a six-storey tenement in the High Street. The house was built in 1620 and has now been restored to the style of that period. Once again this typically Edinburgh setting will also help stir the imaginations of those whose roots lie in other large Scottish towns among the houses of the merchants.

3. Country house

In the north-east of Scotland, between Aberdeen and Inverurie (2½ miles west of Kintore) is a fine country house, built in the 17th century. It has an interesting old-world garden and contains a small museum with a collection of Scottish kitchen antiques. Open between May and September by arrangement, the house is included in the Scottish Tourist Board's *1001 Things to See.*

4. Glasgow Merchant

Glasgow's answer to Edinburgh's Gladstones Land is perhaps Provands Lordship, the oldest house in the City, built before Columbus had gathered together enough cash to go west. It is now an impressive museum with 17th-century furniture.

5. Life in Dumfries

At the other end of Scotland, Dumfries has done wonders with the Old Bridge House, built in 1662, and furnished the rooms in period style to give a picture of life in the town over the intervening centuries.

COTTAGES OF THE HIGHLANDS AND ISLANDS

The bridge between "domestic" museums and those concerned with the work of our forebears is made by the museums of Highlands and Islands life, where the cottage was also the work-place of the crofter and his family.

1. The Highland Folk Museum

If you can only take in one of these fascinating centres try the Highland Folk Museum at Kingussie, an open air complex which you can visit all the year round. It is situated on the main Perth-Inverness road, about 12 miles south west of Aviemore. It includes an 18th-century shooting lodge, a Black House from Lewis, a Clack Mill and exhibits of farming equipment. Inside you'll find find displays including a barn, a dairy, a stable and an exhibition illustrating the life of Highland tinkers. And if you want to see just what your Highland ancestors wore, fought with, sat on or played with, this is for you.

2. Caithness crofting

Very many Scots in North America, Australia and New Zealand will trace their roots back to Caithness and Sutherland, the scene of so many clearances. At Caithness, on the A9 between Helmsdale and Wick, Laidhay Caithness Croft, open from Easter to September, will show just what sort of life those Scots were leaving. An early 18th-century croft complex has been conserved complete with stable house and byre under a single thatched roof. The complex is furnished throughout in the furniture of the period.

3. Isle of Lewis

Lewis has two particularly important points to visit if you are to get a feel for the lives of the crofters and fishermen. An evocative Black House at Arnol, constructed without mortar and roofed with thatch, shows a central peat fire and a number of authentic furnishings. Not far away is the superb

Shawbost Museum where I found my whalebone stools—begun by the local schoolchildren and expanded into a higgledy-piggledy collection of the minutiae of crofting life.

4. Shetland

There is a fine croft house at Dunrossness, 25 miles south of Lerwick, where a complete thatched croft complex has been carefully restored with a mid-19th century thatched croft house and steading, complete with contemporary furnishings. A water mill nearby is worth a visit. Supplement the impact of the croft house with a visit to the fine museum open all year round at Lower Hillhead in Lerwick. It has four galleries dealing with archaeology, art and textiles, folk life and shipping.

5. The Cumbraes

Garrison House in Millport houses the Museum of the Cumbraes, particularly strong on Victorian and Edwardian times when the islands were an integral part of the cruising holiday scene in the West of Scotland.

6. Skye

Perhaps the most evocative name in the Scottish islands, Skye too has its Black House and Water Mill to the west of Dunvegan. A feature of the crofter's house is a replica whisky still!

And extend your trip on Skye to take in the Kilmuir Croft Museum north of Portree, with exhibits which include a wall bed and an array of domestic and farming implements.

7. Mull

Just south of Dervaig, an attractive stone-built byre has been converted to provide a museum of crofting life on Mull, using lifelike figures and a sound commentary.

Other island museums include: the *Bute* Museum at Rothesay, the *South Uist* Folk Museum, housed in a traditional thatched cottage, and, perhaps the best of them all, the Museum of *Islay* Life established in an old Victorian United Free Church building.

FARMING LIFE

1. Agriculture in the north-east

If your ancestors came from north-east Scotland and were farmers, make for the Adamston Agricultural Museum, just south of Huntly. You have to make an appointment (details in *1001 Things to See)* and will be able to see a collection of more than 450 agricultural implements, hand tools, kitchen equipment and farm machinery.

2. Angus two centuries ago

Further south, the rich farming area of Angus is represented by Kirkwynd Cottages, a row of six 17th-century cottages with stone slabbed roofs, containing relics of domestic and agricultural life in the county in the 19th century and earlier. May to September opening or by request.

3. Communal tenancy farm

Just south of Inveraray, you will find the very imaginative Auchindrain Museum, a fascinating example of a communal tenancy farm, with traditional dwellings and barns dating from the late 18th and early 19th century. Furnishings and implements are on display and the land around is worked using traditional methods.

4. Highland estate

The working of a Highland estate was a very specialised form of agriculture—if it was one which involved your ancestors, Braeloine Visitor Centre at Glen Tanar near Aboyne sets out to present the farming, forestry and land use development of the estate.

5. Life in Fife

Perhaps one of the most varied counties of Scotland is Fife with its varied span of industries, from coal to damask, from linoleum to fishing. The Fife Folk Museum at Ceres has a fine setting in an old 17th-century Weigh House near an old bridge in an attractive village. It concentrates on the agricultural and domestic past of Fife life. And don't omit to walk to the nearby church and see the horse-show gallery.

6. Down to Dumfries

Maxwelton House dates back to the 14th/15th century and gains its fame as a stronghold and as birthplace of the inspiring Annie Laurie. It contains a museum of early kitchen, dairy and small farming implements.

7. Turning out scones

A meal and flour mill at Blair Atholl is still carrying on the tradition set in its early days 200 years ago—turning out a small quantity of oatmeal which is sold locally and flour which goes into the small wholemeal bakery. You can even get lessons in making your own scones and oatcakes! There are other working mills at Aberfeldy and Prestonmill, near East Linton.

8. Thanks to Robbie

The fact that the national poet was also a farmer gives those in search of farming museums an added bonus. Many of the superb Robert Burns museums tell the visitor as much about the farmer as about the poet. The various centres are linked into a Burns Heritage Trail. Start as Burns did at the cottage in Alloway—and you'll learn a lot about the life of your farming forebears.

DOWN TO THE SEA IN SHIPS

With her clusters of islands and seemingly infinite coastline, Scotland (and your ancestors) could never get far away from the business of fishing and all its allied trades. The following reflect that relationship:

1. Scottish Fisheries Museum

At Anstruther Harbour, in St Ayles Land, a building with a charter dated 1318, a fascinating collection has been built up of items illustrating the fisherman's life at home and at sea, historical and modern. The museum also contains a marine aquarium and is restoring a 70-ft sailing "Fifie." At the east pier in the same village you can go aboard the North Carr Lightship—a floating museum and well worth a visit.

2. Whales and Scotland

Peterhead's Arbuthnot Museum covers the development of fishing and whaling and has a large number of Arctic exhibits. And, to show that not even museums have to dwell on the past, it has a section on offshore oil as befits one of Scotland's major beneficiaries of North Sea activity.

3. More whales

Dundee was an important whaling base and the Broughty Castle museum reflects this past with harpoons, darts, knives, axes and scrimshaws galore.

4. Objects, models, paintings

Cutting across to Buckie, you will find a maritime museum which shows clothing, gear and models relating to the fishing industry. Interestingly, the Anson gallery houses a collection of water colours on the development of fishing in Scotland.

5. Herring etc

Further along the Moray Firth, Nairn Fishertown Museum has a collection of articles and photographs connected with the fishing heritage of the area—and with herring fishing industries during the steam drifter era. Good coverage too of the domestic life of the fisher folk.

6. Lighthouses

The life and work of many Scots who manned the lighthouses is represented in Arbroath's Signal Tower.

THE BASIC INDUSTRIES

Scotland's mining and extractive industries developed early—and many of you may have traced back your roots to areas where these hard and demanding jobs were concentrated. After being ignored for a very long time, these industries are now receiving some long overdue historical attention.

1. Slate quarrying

Along with North Wales, the West Coast of Scotland was one of the centres to provide slate for the great house-building projects of the 19th century. The Glencoe and North Lorn Museum in Glencoe village deals with the famous local industry as well as with the more romantic activities of Bonnie Prince Charlie. The museum is housed in a number of thatched cottages.

2. Swinging the lead

Lead was another valuable raw material found in Scotland and localised to a large extent in the Wanlockhead area. The Museum of the Scottish Lead Mining Industry is there (open April to September) and bristling with mining and social relics housed in a cottage. In the open-air section, you'll find a lead mine beam engine, smelt and but-and-ben cottages. You can even go down a lead mine and see conditions at first hand. And if you have tracked your ancestors back to the lead industry, there's a local library with books and records of the reading society which was founded in 1756. The Allan Ramsay library at nearby Leadhills also has a lot to offer.

3. Old Paraffin Young

The oil industry has returned after a long spell away from home to the country where it all started—although the early oil was paraffin, obtained from the shale of West Lothian. A special trail takes you around the area, revealing the life of James "Paraffin" Young and the industry which he founded. The trail is aimed for the car driver, with signs en route to guide you and your thoughts. If your ancestors came from Pumpherston, West Calder, Winchburgh, Broxburn or Bathgate—they may very well have played a part in Young's empire.

4. Centuries of coal

Of all the materials hewn from the soil of Scotland, coal has probably involved more of your ancestors, spread over a greater part of the country than any other. The museum of the industry is housed at Prestongrange in East Lothian, only eight miles east of Edinburgh. On the site of a colliery with 800 years of recorded running history (just think about that!), the museum has an impressive centre-piece in the form of an 1874 Cornish Beam Pumping Engine and its five-floor Engine House. The former Power House is now an exhibition hall with many mining artefacts, plans, photographs and documents. There are also two steam locomotives, a hundred-year-old steam navvy and a colliery winding machine on site.

(You will also find areas devoted to coal miners in the museums of *Kirkcaldy* and *Blantyre*, the latter the Livingstone National Memorial).

TRANSPORTS OF DELIGHT

In the nineteenth century, which will take up much of your family research, transport was a major activity in Scotland—not just using it, but laying the foundations for it, building the equipment, and of course running it.

1. Canals

When the Union Canal was opened in 1822, part of its infrastructure involved a large stable block (to keep the horse-power happy) at *Linlithgow*. Today, those stables house records, photographs, an audio-visual display and relics of the history of the canal (not forgetting a lot of the wildlife around it). You can also go on a trip by canal boat (Ratho and Linlithgow) to get the feel of one of the wonders of the early 19th century. *Grangemouth* Museum also concentrates on the canals of central Scotland, including canal tools and a model lock—plus exhibits relating to the *Charlotte Dundas,* the world's first practical steamship.

2. Railways

In addition to the great museums of Glasgow and Edinburgh whose working models and actual exhibits have fascinated small boys of all ages for generations, the Scottish Railway Preservation Society, based at *Falkirk*, offers a fine display of restored railway vehicles. If you want to experience travel on a steam-engine you can do so on private lines at Strathspey, Lochty and Alford.

3. Carriages

St Cuthbert's (Edinburgh's Co-operative Association) has a fine collection of horse-drawn carriages—which your forebears may have built, driven or ridden in, while the City's Transport Museum also has a broad display of transport in the capital over the centuries.

4. Transport in general

The Daddy of them all is of course the great Glasgow Museum of Transport—trams, buses, motor cars (including the oldest in Scotland), horse-drawn vehicles, fire engines and bicycles abounding—and even a collection of ship models.

THE TEXTILE INDUSTRIES

Barely a corner of Scotland was without its spinning and weaving activity and specialisation—and it would be quite difficult to get back to the eighteenth century without coming across at least one forebear "in the business."

1. Handloom weaving

If you get back as far as the 18th century, your forebears would certainly have been doing their weaving by hand in a cottage. At *Kilbarchan*, west of Paisley, a cottage has been preserved as a home typical of the period when Kilbarchan was a thriving centre of handloom weaving.

2. Linen and damask

The weaving of fine linen and damask objects was the specialisation which made *Dunfermline* industry famous. It is naturally well represented in the town museum. *Kinross,* not too far up the road, also has a section on linen manufacture in its museum.

3. Cotton spinning

One of the many aspects of the local area's activity on display in *Blantyre's* Livingstone National Memorial is cotton spinning.

4. Spinning and weaving by hand

Over on the west coast, on the southern edge of *Oban*, you can see at McDonald's Mill an exhibition of the story of spinning and weaving—and actual demonstrations of how these types were done by hand.

5. New Lanark

Perhaps the finest example of Scotland's preserved industrial past is at New Lanark, the setting of Robert Owen's advanced experiments in establishing a model manufacturing community.

6. Paisley wear

Scottish Paisley design has found its way to all corners of the world—and the industry is well displayed at the *Paisley* Museum with lots of superb shawls.

7. Wool textiles

The Scottish Museum of Wool Textiles is housed at *Walkerburn,* between Peebles and Galashiels, at the mill of Henry Ballantyne. The display presents the growth of the textile trade, with many interesting exhibits—and demonstrations of hand spinning.

METALWORKING

Iron-smelting is represented in the restored remains of a charcoal furnace for iron smelting which was established in 1753 and worked until 1874. Situated at Bonawe, 12 miles east of Oban, this can be viewed from the outside and is the finest example of such a complex.

TOWN LIFE

The trades of the towns are well displayed at Biggar, in the Gladstone Court Street Museum. This is in the unique form of an "indoor" street museum of shops and windows. Grocer, photographer, dressmaker, bank, school, library, ironmonger, chemist, china merchant and telephone exchange are featured. An open-air museum is being developed and a 17th-century farmhouse rebuilt. A reconstructed Edwardian shop also figures in *Kirkcaldy*'s Museum. At Fochabers in the north-east, Old Baxter's shop offers a similar chance to step back into the past.

Shoemaking was, in view of the difficulty in automating such an essential industry, a trade followed by many. There were for example at the time of the 1851 Census well over 30,000 in Scotland! The fact that Burns immortalised one of these—Souter Johnnie in "Tam o' Shanter"—has been instrumental in giving the shoemakers a museum of their own. Souter Johnnie's House in Kirkoswald, not far from Maybole, is a thatched cottage which was the home of village cobbler (souter) John Davidson at the end of the 18th century. The cottage now contains a selection of Burnsiana—and an exhibition of the contemporary tools of the cobbler's craft.

SERVING THE COMMUNITY

The host of local authority services which now influence our lives at so many stages are comparatively new—and the people employed in them equally short on heritage. But you may be surprised to find that there are in Scotland museums to give you something of the background to:

1. Policemen

At the Strathclyde Police Headquarters in Glasgow, there is a small police museum showing the history of the police service in Scotland—along with some articles from a variety of crime cases!

2. Firemen

As befits the city which "invented" the municipal fire-fighting force, Edinburgh has a museum complete with old uniforms, equipment and engines. This is one business where demands cannot be predicted in advance so there may be times when you can't see around as everyone is out fighting fires. The museum is named the Braidwood and Rushbrook Fire Museum. Braidwood, having set up the first Fire Brigade in the 1820s, then went off to London to show them it could be done there too.

3. Prison-officers

On the site of Jedburgh Castle a modern "reform" jail was built in 1825. Rooms have been interestingly reconstructed to recreate the "reformed" system of the early 19th century. Should interest you, whether your forebears were here as workers or as prisoners!

4. Social workers

I have discovered that Scotland has in Milngavie near Glasgow the world's only museum of social work. There are 2500 slides of the 19th and early 20th century, and 5000 volumes in the reference library! Again, whether your forebears gave out the charity or received it, this has potential.

DISTILLING

Ask a hundred tourists to name a Scottish industry—and distilling will almost certainly come to mind in the majority of cases. It was never an industry which employed vast numbers of Scots (but it is worth remembering that there were many ancillary trades from coopers to coppersmiths that may have been pursued by your forebears). It is, however, an industry which is well displayed. You will find actual working distilleries open and welcoming, and eager to display some of the secrets of the art and mystery. *Dufftown*'s own museum deals with the vital Banffshire industry and from there you can follow the Whisky Trail and take in a number of famous distilleries including Glendronach, Glenfarclas, Glenfiddich,

Glen Grant, Glenlivet, and at Keith the oldest of them all, Strathisla. Off the main Banffshire trail, you'll find other distilleries well worth a visit. Look out for them.

THE CLAN MUSEUMS

Perhaps the image of Scotland which gets the most airing on the international scene is the picture of a rigid, clan-oriented society all living, if we are to believe those maps and tea-towels, in clearly defined "reservations." The truth is far from that, but the existence of the clans was a very real element in the lives of your ancestors Highland—and you may gain an insight into the times from a visit to some of the relevant clan museums. Here is a selection:

1. Clan Tartan Centre

This centre at Aviemore offers an exhibition, reference library and audio-visual display—and even the computerised tracing of clan links, complete with a commentary in four languages.

2. Clan Donald Centre

Based at Armadale Castle, the centre houses a museum of the history of the Macdonalds and the Lords of the Isles. The setting is particularly beautiful.

3. Clan Donnachaidh Museum

The Clan takes in Reid, Robertson, MacConnachie, Duncan, MacInroy and others—which is a fair chunk of Scots. Particularly strong on items associated with the Jacobite Risings of 1715 and 1745. The museum is to be found four miles west of Blair Atholl.

4. Clan Gunn Museum

The newly opened museum is located in the mid-18th-century parish church of Latheron on the A9, before it reaches Wick.

5. Clan Macpherson Museum

The clan museum has a range of relics and memorials including the black chanter, green banner and charmed sword, Prince Charles Edward Stewart relics and a magnificent silver centrepiece. You'll find it at Newtonmore, 15 miles south of Aviemore.

6. Strathnaver Museum

While this is not specifically a clan museum, it is right in the heart of the Clan Mackay country and is associated with the Sutherland Clearances to which many overseas Scots may well be able to establish links.

A SCOTTISH SOLDIER OR TWO

Fighting has always been a major Scottish industry, with the nation providing over the centuries quality fighters not only to Britain but also to a strange mix of foreign powers. At home, the fighting tradition has been firmly built on the great Scottish regiments. While the reader who traces ancestors who were professional soldiers may well have to go to London to find the details of an individual, it is to Scotland that he must look to learn something of the regiments with which his forebear fought.

1. Gordon Highlanders

The regimental headquarters in *Aberdeen* is open all the year round and offers fine displays relating to the Gordon Highlanders' varied campaigns. There are collections of uniforms, colours and banners, silver and medals and a library with historical material and photograph albums.

2. Argyll and Sutherland Highlanders

The setting of *Stirling* Castle will take some beating—this fine regimental museum does full justice to it. Particularly strong in its medal collection.

3. Black Watch

This famous regiment has its headquarters and museum in Balhousie Castle in *Perth*. The exhibits offer a dramatic way of following the development of this famous regiment from 1740 to the present day.

4. The Cameronians

The Cameronians (Scottish Rifles) Regimental Museum is in *Hamilton* and, in addition to the usual regimental exhibits, is especially strong on the Covenanting times.

5. Royal Scots

The Royal Scots, the Royal Regiment, have their museum at *Edinburgh* Castle. An impressive display of pictures, badges, brassware and other historical relics of the oldest regiment in the British Army awaits you.

6. Queen's Own Highlanders

Fort George, near *Inverness*, was begun in 1748 as a result of the fright caused by the 1745 Jacobite Rising, and is one of Europe's finest late artillery fortifications. It houses the museum of the Queen's Own Highlanders.

7. Royal Highland Fusiliers

Glasgow is the base for the regiment in which are concentrated the traditions of the Royal Scots Fusiliers, The Highland Light Infantry and the Royal Highland Fusiliers. Fine records of fine histories.

8. The Scottish Horse Museum

Scottish Horse was a Yeomanry Regiment and at the

Military heritage at the Gordon Highlanders Museum, Aberdeen

Cross, *Dunkeld*, you will find exhibits, uniforms, photographs, maps and, most significantly for the ancestor-hunter, rolls of all those who served in Scottish Horse.

9. The Scottish United Services Museum

Edinburgh Castle houses the greatest of the military museums—easy to get at and comprehensive in the extreme.

URBAN LIFE

By the nineteenth century an increasing number of Scots—and that includes your forebears—were moving from the land into the towns and cities. You will get a good impression of urban life from the Scottish city museums:

1. Edinburgh

Edinburgh life down the ages is probably best portrayed in the Huntly House Museum in the Canongate.

2. Glasgow

Scotland's largest city has its museum of local history in the People's Palace, opened in 1898 and telling the story of Glasgow from 1175 onwards—although strongest in the period where your ancestor-hunting will have concentrated.

3. Dundee

To get the overall feel of Dundee life, you really need to see the two museums – the main Museum strong on social history, especially nineteenth century, and the Barrack Street Museum good on transport, including ships and shipping and on Victorian schooldays.

4. Stirling

On the Castle Esplanade, Stirling has a Landmark Visitor

Centre to provide you with a very modern multi-screen, audio-visual insight into the history of Stirling.

5. Perth

Open all the year round, Perth Art Gallery and Museum houses collections of local history exhibits and also holds a changing programme of temporary exhibitions.

LOCAL LINKS

In addition to professions and trades, regiments and industries, you will have placed your forebears within precise locations within Scotland—and this means that the local museums will have a great deal to offer in terms of telling you about the life of the community in which your forebears lived. There are too many first-rate museums to list them all, but you should see if the area you are interested in is covered by a good museum focussed on local matters. Here are some of the significant Scottish local museums outside the many that I have already listed as dealing with specific topics as well as covering a defined geographical area:

Banff, Banchory (a small display in the old Council Chambers), *Bo'ness* (especially strong on the local manufactures of pottery, cast-iron and salt-pan implements), *Brechin* (housed in the library), *Burntisland*, *Coupar Angus, Dingwall* (in the fine 18th century Town House, strong on the career of local hero Sir Hector MacDonald), *Dumfries* (covering the whole of the Solway area, based on a 200-year-old windmill and featuring a camera obscura), *Falkirk* (good on local pottery, clocks, weapons and Victoriana), *Glenesk* (nicely folk-oriented), *Haddington* (a small display, but here the whole town is a museum and evocative of the inhabitants' past), *Hawick* (in Wilton Lodge Park, superb setting, excellent on Border relics plus good art exhibitions), *Inverkeithing*, *Inverurie* (thematic exhibitions three times a year), *Irvine, Kinross* (good on local peat-cutting and military activities), *Largs* (local history books and photographs), *Paisley, Saltcoats* (excellent on local manufacture of salt and export of coal to Ireland), *Sanquhar, Stonehaven* (fishing in particular, but a fine building too which has served as storehouse, prison and lodging house in its time), *Stewartry* (museum at Kirkcudbright, with the additional interest for any US visitors that the founder of their Navy, John Paul Jones, was born nearby), and *Wigtown* (spotlight on dairy farming and local explorer Sir John Ross).

It is not possible to produce a definitive list of all of the museums which might add something to your investigations into your Scottish roots. Current Scottish Tourist Board publications such as the unbeatable *1001 Things to See* (complete with fine, linked map), will give you details of the museums, by area and by subject, as well as letting you know up-to-date prices and times of admission.

BASE SEVEN

Doing it from a distance

Doing it from a distance—an approach to tracking down your Scots ancestors if you can't get to Edinburgh—or even to Scotland

THE CO-TENANTS of these British Isles are quite easy to distinguish the one from the other. Eight Englishmen ship-wrecked on a desert island would sit there silently, waiting to be introduced. Eight Irishmen would sit on the sand, waiting for the cement to arrive. Eight Welshmen would form a Rugby scrum (with, as my Scots friends keep reminding me, seven of them in an offside position). Eight Scots would of course form seven Caledonian Societies.

The fact of the matter is that the Scots seem to have been cast up on more numerous, more distant and more varied shores than almost any other nationality, and the result of this and that habit of setting up Caledonian Societies is that there are people from every corner of the world who see themselves as Scottish and their roots as undeniably tartan.

For them, the main theme of this book—the mouth-watering treasures that await them throughout the length and breadth of Scotland, and at the east end of Princes Street, Edinburgh, in particular—may seem a little irrelevant. This chapter is written especially for them—and indeed for many Scots who cannot get down to Edinburgh and devote days or weeks to this ancestor-hunting kick.

Even if you are doing it from a distance, the principles outlined in this book remain valid.

The first step is to find out as much as possible from your own sources. Go and read the section of Base One again and you will see how to set about amassing the type of information that is even more essential to anyone who is not able to carry out the research in Scotland in person.

In particular, look out for specific and clearly dated links with Scotland.

When did your ancestor leave Scotland? Arrive in your present country? Do you have any records which can help to answer these points?

In addition to the family interviews/letters mentioned in this book, think in particular of the following:

1. Are there any records in my present country which give details of the Scottish link?

- A will made in Australia by your grandfather may mention brothers and sisters still left in Scotland.
- Scots leaving home in the nineteenth century were not required to file any details here in Scotland. Catching a boat across the ocean was no different, as far as Government records were concerned, from catching a bus today. Records do, however, often exist at the other end. Ships' passenger lists were often filed at the port of entry. Governments often kept records of immigration, which can compensate for Scotland's lack of emigration records.
- Death records of, say, a Scot who came to Canada and died there may carry the name of his parents. If so, this is a very valuable piece of information, along with any details of his place of birth. (These are details which may even have been carried in the immigration records).

2. Are there any less formal clues to the Scottish connection?

- Scots often named their house in the new home after a farm or village or area where they lived in Scotland. Any records of your forebears' first years in their new home may indicate this.

- Are there any family traditions which could throw a light on Scotland? For the most part the bulk of family traditions are poor guides to reality, but it is not always the case. Often, an important element is handed down by word of mouth and where the details are precise enough this can be a help.

3. Are there any of the sort of documents mentioned in Base One which bridge the gap between Scotland and the new home?

Books? Diaries? Photographs? Old photographs may not have a background which will enable you to locate the setting, but commercial photographers usually have their mark somewhere on the surround or even back of the print. If an old fading print bears the stamp of, say, "Macfarlane, Photographer, Crieff," that could provide a pointer to the family origins.

4. Did you know anything of the family that were left behind?

Let us suppose that your grandfather came from Scotland and died in New Zealand and that his records in New Zealand give no indications of his parents or birthplace in Scotland. Did he have any brothers or sisters who did not go to New Zealand with him? What were their names? Were they older or younger than he was? More importantly, do you have any precise details of when they married? Or when they died? If you knew that his sister Isabella died in Dundee in 1897, that information would enable you to get from the Scottish records the same information as if your grandfather had died there.

5. Do you know anything of the Church to which your Scots ancestor belonged?

There was usually a tradition of church-going which passed

on from parents to children. Particularly when looking back beyond the civil records, it is important to know which church was likely to have kept records of Births, Marriages and Deaths. As I have mentioned, the established Church of Scotland records are the ones kept by the Registrar-General in his old, pre-1855 material.

6. What was the profession or trade of your Scots ancestor?

This could provide one of the most valuable guides to tracking down a family (and not only in helping confirm that the Ian Macleod you track down in Scotland is the same one that you knew about in Nova Scotia!). The professions have their own very fine directories, so that if the emigrating Scot was a doctor, minister or lawyer, you have a very good chance of finding him. Similarly, if he attended university in Scotland, it would be handy to see what information is carried on him in the directories of graduates. The same would apply to any school directories which may exist. (See Base Six for these details).

It is not only the professions, however, for whom there are fine, informative records. The Army records housed in London, provided you have some idea of the regiment, can give much information of value to the ancestor-hunter. Moreover, almost every trade or occupation found its way into the town directories which cover most of Scotland's cities from the early 19th century onwards. So if your ancestor was a bookseller or coachhirer, a bootmaker or a policeman, in Dundee or Glasgow, Edinburgh or Perth, this is invaluable as an aid to tracking him down.

7. Did the family own any land, no matter how small, in Scotland?

The great Sasine registers list the owners (but not the tenants) of all land in Scotland. If you have a date and an address, it is possible to extract information from the Sasines which could help build up extra information on your family.

The main aim of all this activity is to build up as much information as possible on your Scottish links, because the quality and quantity of the information which it is possible to extract from the records depends to a large extent on just what information you start with.

Look again at the section on New Register House, Base Two. In summary, these are the requirements needed to tap into those three great hoards of information:

1. Births Marriages and Deaths after 1855

To get to an entry you need a name and date, for a birth, a marriage or a death. A place would also help out, as would occupation or names of parents. These extras are important when the name is a common one.

2. The Census returns, 1841-1891

You must have a family name and an address which is applicable at or near one of the decennial census dates.

3. Pre-1855, Old Parochial Records

You must have in addition to family names and approximate dates a parish in which the baptisms, banns and burials took place.

Without these basic details, the chances of a successful search are eliminated or severely reduced.

But let's get back to the campaign. You, sir, there in Moose Jaw, or you, madam, sunning yourself in Lochinver! How can *you* get all this ancestor-hunting under way?

There are basically *three* methods at your disposal:

1. Ancestors by post

You can build up a wealth of information, by ordering, from the Registrar-General copies of all the key documents which are needed to build up your family tree. This is:

a. *Expensive*—you, unlike the searcher on the spot who can take notes from a record, have to purchase a copy of the document. The charges are reasonable (you'll find them listed in Appendix I) but they mount up.

b. Slow—you have to wait for two postal services (you to the Registrar-General, he to you) with a searching and processing time in between. (You might console yourself that the Sassenach, banned from the documents themselves, has no real alternative to this one). You usually can't get on with the next stage until you have noted the details carried on the first document.

c. Dependent on accurate information—the Registrar-General's staff are not involved in the business of research. They will find for you and copy an entry for which you provide enough information to make its location feasible. If you want a death certificate of George Macrae, who died in Inverness in 1876, they will provide it. If you want a certificate for a George Macrae who died somewhere north of Inverness, between 1870 and 1878, they are less likely to provide it.

Nevertheless this is a feasible means of setting about the initial research. And it does have the benefit of providing you with copies or photostats of the actual documents which log your ancestors' history.

2. Using the professional searchers

If the staff of the Registrar-General are not in the business of personalised ancestry research, there are others who are—providing the on-the-spot investigation, speeded one may add by an expertise and flair for the records which cannot be acquired overnight, for people who want to find out more about their Scottish roots. Naturally, with the concentration of most records in Edinburgh, this is very much a capital city profession!

The professional searchers represent a nice blend of private enterprise and Government initiative, as there are a number of individual operators (some are listed in Appendix VI) as well as the non-profit-making, but self-funding Scots Ancestry Research Society.

The Scots Ancestry Research Society was established in 1945 by Tom Johnston, the most effective Secretary of State Scotland has managed to acquire and a man to whom Scots owe much. He set up the Society, in the words of its current pamphlet, to "assist persons of Scottish blood to trace facts about their ancestors in Scotland." The Society has seven researchers on its books (able to draft in others if the need arises), and a highly qualified board of specialists.

The Society's experience (it has handled more than 50,000 overseas enquiries) is representative of the sort of work the professional researchers are required to undertake—and the sort of problems with which they are faced.

The problems seem to be summed up in one phrase—"not enough detail." That is one reason for my placing so much emphasis on the spade-work which has to be done *before* you send off asking someone to start work on your behalf.

A look at what the Society's researchers set out to do—and how much they are likely to charge you for it!—will give you a rough picture of the service offered by all of Scotland's professional researchers.

If you, sir, still sitting in Moose Jaw, would like the Society to get to work on your behalf, you send a fee to get on to the Society's books (currently £10 or $25 US). You, madam, in Lochinver, need pay VAT as well, taking it up to £11.50.

You should also enclose an International Reply Coupon (from Moose Jaw) or a stamped addressed envelope (from Lochinver).

You then have to fill in the registration form. (For the special use of readers we include a tear-out page in this book which the Society has agreed to accept). This asks for quite a bit of information, but if you have more do not hesitate to include it on a separate sheet.

The Registration Fee gets you on to the books, and the Registration Form authorises the Society to carry out on your behalf research up to a maximum of £80 (plus VAT for the lady in Lochinver) or about $200 US. This is a maximum figure—in many cases the actual bill comes to less than that. If you are feeling flush—or even spending your great-uncle's legacy and feel some of it should go on this roots binge—you can stipulate a higher maximum.

So the beavers get down to work. What are you going to get for that money?

There is, as you may have guessed from our two case histories (pages 81 to 104), no way of answering that question in advance. In essence the researchers are trying to build up one line only (the paternal) unless you ask otherwise (and that costs more). They will, for example, try and track down your great-grandfather's brothers and sisters, but not his in-laws.

The elements which influence just what you will get for your money are numerous but mainly the following:

1. *Information*: the more detailed and precise the information you can give, the more likely is it that the searchers will come up with a lot for that £80.
2. *Luck*: again our case-histories have underlined the role of luck in these searches—unusual names and, in the earlier records, the quality (or even the existence) of parish records.
3. *Family size*—your searchers aim to track down the paternal line and all children of each direct descent marriage. Now if you, sir, in Moose Jaw come up with a great-grandfather who had thirteen children, and you, madam, in Lochinver, with one who had only one child—your grandfather—then there are two likely sequences:

- You, sir, will get a large number of relatives on your list, but may feel a little disappointed at the number of generations the searchers have managed to get through.
- You, madam, may be very pleased at just how many generation bands the searchers have turned up, but a little disappointed at the lack of "breadth."

The tall spindly family tree or the dense squat family bush—you will certainly get a lot of effort from the searchers and they will be trying their hardest to make sure you are pleased with what you get for your money.

Incidentally, if the searchers come up with an "ancestor" that they cannot fix categorically from documentary evidence, they will end the search and let you know how things stand. You may then accept that while the link cannot be proved it is highly probable—and ask them to continue from the "ancestor."

The important point to emphasise at this stage is that unlike our case histories, their work will be ranging not only over the records of New Register House, but also through the legal, land, testamentary material and much else of the neighbouring Scottish Records Office, plus the many directories of apprentices and tradesmen, gravestones and school-rolls, doctors and graduates, churchmen and burgesses.

3. A combination of 1 and 2

It is also worth considering a combination of 1 and 2, where this is possible. You deal directly with the Registrar-General, ordering key documents and building up a partial family tree which you can at some stage hand over to the professionals for their contribution. Similarly—and this is a dimension which has only emerged in recent years—you may get your work from the professional searchers and then do the laborious searching of the OPRs on your own. But, ah, I hear you mutter, the whole point of this exercise is that I *can't* get to Register House where he has told me *all* the OPRs are kept.

This strange change of tack can be put down to the Mormons, the Salt Lake City-based Church of Jesus Christ of Latter Day Saints. With their great emphasis on genealogical work, the Mormons have established at Salt Lake City the world's greatest centre of genealogical information, most of it on microfilm and much of it stored on computer and retrievable through the most amazing Computer File Index.

In the context of searching for Scottish ancestors, the great importance is that the Old Parochial Registers are available on microfilm through a number of Mormon library sources. This could mean that you, sir, would be able to study the pre-1855 records outside of Scotland itself. If you are interested in pursuing this possibility, you should try and find the location of the nearest Mormon library and make enquiries there.

It is important to realise that Mormon work on micro-filming and storing Scottish records has been confined to the Old Parochial Records and does not extend to either the census returns or the post-1855 civil registrations.

All the very best of luck with your attempts to do it from a distance. You will certainly enjoy the experience and it may encourage you, sir, to make that trip from Moose Jaw to Scotland, not just to wade through the records, but perhaps to visit those places identified for you in the copies sent to you by the Registrar-General or in the report prepared by your professional searchers. And you, madam, in Lochinver, may think it worth coming down to Edinburgh for a couple of days after all!

BASE EIGHT

Back home—getting it all down

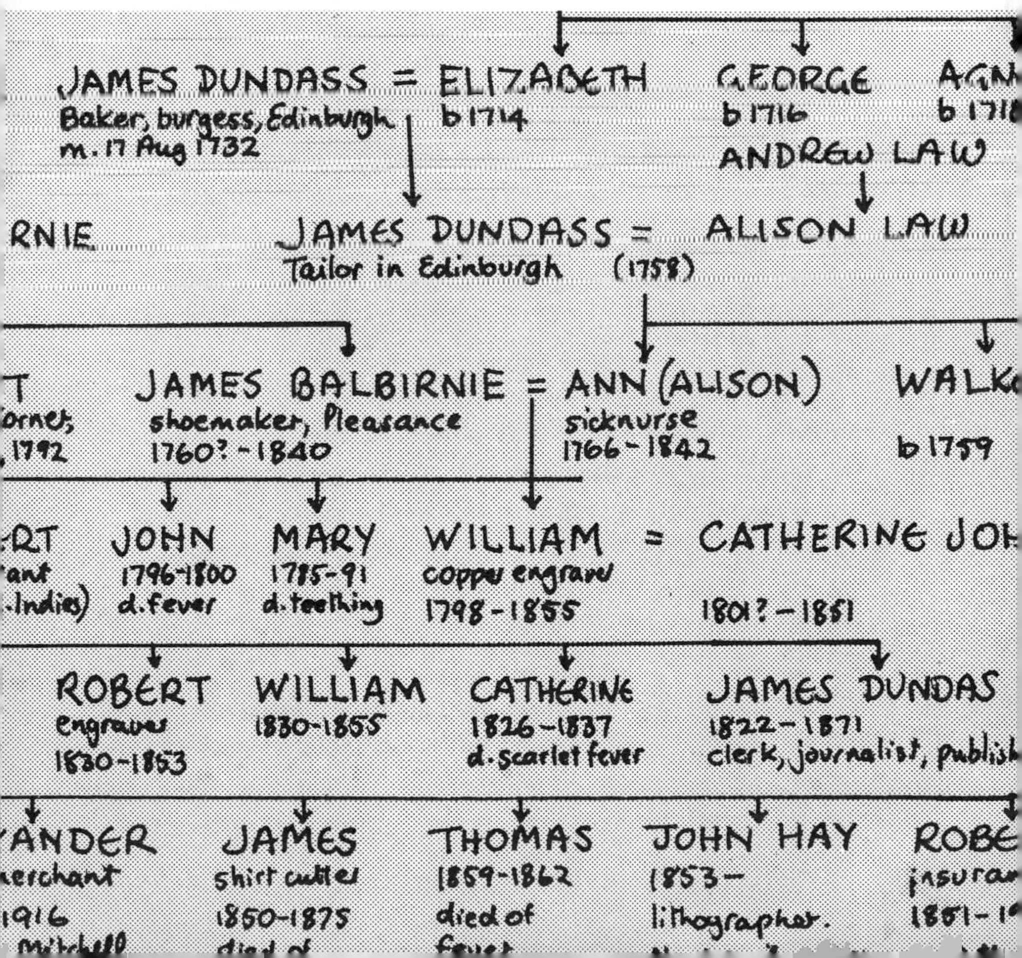

It is always tempting, but rarely justifiable to link individuals of whom we know little to events of major historical significance. We can however safely assume that the Balbirnies joined with their fellow citizens in reacting to two specific happenings of the 1820s.

Two generations of Balbirnies surely joined in the enormous crowds which flocked to see George IV, the first Hanoverian monarch to visit Scotland in a famous Royal progress masterminded by Sir Walter Scott.

With equal certainty, we can assume that in the latter part of the decade three generations of Balbirnies, living in the claustrophobic confines of the Old Town, shuddered to the tales of body-snatching which led relatives to mount guard over the fresh graves of their dear departed and which culminated in 1828 with the Burke and Hare affair. These two ruffians, not content with the chancy and unpredictable revenue of waiting for and then selling corpses, decided to go into production as well as distribution - and landed up on a gruesome murder charge. Hare turned King's Evidence - and Burke landed up in January 1829 at the end of a rope. The well-attended public hanging took place opposite the Balbirnie home !

The Balbirnies, young and old, managed to get through the great cholera epidemic of 1832 which swept through the Old Town killing 600 people in six months, some in the very building where they lived. Five years later however the young daughter Catherine died of scarlet fever at the age of ten.

An example of a family history, mixing local detail with the family's growth

Now that you have got all that material, what do you do with it?

OVER THE weeks (months? years?), you will have amassed an enormous hoard of information and at the end of asking a thousand and one questions of who, when and where, you are left with only two: when do I stop, and what do I do then?

The first is perhaps the simplest because there is no real answer to it. Genealogy, as I said at the beginning, is a jigsaw puzzle which gets bigger and bigger and which never throws up a piece with an unequivocal straight edge to let you know you've reached the end. And so there is always a temptation to keep searching. At some stage you must resist that temptation and say to yourself: I have reached the stage where I have so much information that I must try and get it down on paper in a manageable form as a record that can clarify my work from my own point of view and that can pass on the fruits of that work to others. Console yourself with the knowledge that this is not an irrevocable decision and any facts which come to light afterwards can be incorporated in all but the most polished finished version.

So you've decided to start getting it all down. Pay particular attention to three key aspects:

- putting in order the material you have
- incorporating it into the family tree
- producing a write-up of your findings

Putting in order the material you have collected

The tidy-minded worker will have been keeping a pretty close track of what material he has been accumulating. Now is the time for everyone to try and shuffle those sheets into a logical order, file all the census returns together, mark any cross references on your family or individual sheets. Now is also the time when you should take a careful look at your notepads and information sheets to see if you have missed out any details in transcription or if there are still gaps which can be easily filled.

Building up the family tree

Again, most of you will have been slowly building up a family tree, keeping it simple, using lines and abbreviations as you have seen in the examples in this book. It is now time to try and incorporate all of your material into what is still the most effective way of displaying genealogical information. Each family will pose its own problems as far as layout is concerned, but take a look at history books in your local library and see how other people tackle these challenges.

Get your roughs together and get a clear picture of what your end result should look like. Remember: keep it simple: you are out to produce a device for registering information and passing that information on to others. You are not in the business of producing wallpaper, so cut out the symbolic branches and leafy excesses.

If you intend doing the tree yourself, bear in mind that the job calls for neatness, patience and dedication as much as artistic inspiration. It also calls for some pretty large sheets of paper. If you have any difficulty in local stationers or artists' materials shops, try any local businesses that you think would be handling such sheets—architects, drawing offices, and, best of all, printers especially of newspapers who have ideal layout sheets which they may part with in return for courtesy and a smile.

Modern fibre-tip and allied pens provide some ideal writing implements—but check for permanence as you don't want your family tree to dissolve spectacularly when Aunt Mildred weeps over it in memory of her sister Jessie's details. If you are in the slightest doubt, go for the old well-tried Indian ink. You will also find that sticking to black ink will pay dividends when it comes to reproducing copies for distribution within the family.

It is always worth remembering that there may be other members of the family who may possess the necessary talents to make an even better job of this part of the exercise and who would be delighted to play a small part in putting your talent for research together with their talents for calligraphy.

The family history takes shape

You have gathered from the bald facts of birth, marriage and death the framework, the skeleton, for your family history. You should also somewhere along the line have been fitting that history into the events of the community and nation in which it took place, with local papers, census returns and such-like filling in the details of the grass roots activity and the broader history books telling you something of what was happening in the world around.

You are now ready to build that information into narrative which can be read with interest by other members of the family or (and don't be modest) by people wanting to learn something about a tiny little segment of Scotland's history as represented by one family.

The easiest (and dreariest) thing in the world is to rattle off a list of births, marriages and deaths. Take a look at some of those chapters in the New Testament on the lineage of Jesus and you will be reminded that a chorus of begats is a powerful lullaby indeed.

The following are a few guidelines which might help those of you who are perhaps unused to writing a lengthy continuous report of this type:

- While it may be that the right way to handle your family history is to start at the earliest date and work through to the present day, take a look at your family tree and see if there is an alternative. You may for example have found far more about one generation than another. If that is Generation Band Six, say, but you had actually traced the family back to Band Ten, don't waste time getting to the interesting bit. Start with your key person and sketch in his background as a sort of flashback.
- The more you know about Scotland and its history, the better placed you are to slot your forebears into a period, so try some extra background reading now that you know where your forebears lived and what they did. Try and imagine someone in two hundred years' time trying to piece together a history of a family living in Clydeside in the 1940s and not knowing about World War II—and make sure that that is not what you are trying to do when you look back two centuries.
- Get to know something about the community in which your family lived. Local newspapers for the nineteenth century and the *Statistical Account* for the eighteenth should get you started.
- If you know something of your forebears' occupations, try and find out about what was happening in that trade. Weavers or locomotive-builders, farmers or builders—there are very few people indeed who were working at a job that has been neglected by the academics, writers and publishers of the twentieth century.

It may be that you really have difficulty in getting all this together; the amount of information can often deter even the most experienced writer. Again, look at the possibility that someone in the family may have a bent for narrative and a feeling for history. Collaborate with enthusiasm for the sake of the end product.

Finally, just imagine for a moment that you discovered in a dusty chest a bundle of sheets on which your great-great-grandfather had written down a synopsis of his life: his childhood and friends, games and schools, work and courtship, holidays and hobbies, wife and children. Just feel the glee and ponder. You cannot "create" that treasure that never was, but you can start laying it down for future generations. Set to it and prepare for the family history the contribution which you can make more fully than anyone in the world—the story of your life, a plain, but not too plain, collection of what you would like your great-great-grandson to know about you. Nothing too grand, not a great autobiographical novel. Although, if you do get hooked. . . .

APPENDIX I

New Register House Costs at Summer 1986

A member of staff will search for a specific entry for you—when you have enough information to make identification likely. Any entry from the post-1855 Births, Marriages and Deaths, from the Old Parochial Records or the census returns can then be copied for you at a cost of £5 (search and extract).

If the search does not come up with your entry, you will have to pay up to £2.50 for each five-year period involved in the search.

You yourself or a representative may make a general search over any period for any number of entries on payment of the following daily rates:

In the indexes to the post-1855 BMDs	£5.50
In the parish registers pre-1855	£4.50
In the census returns 1841-1891	£4.50

If your searches are to range over more than one category, the following charges apply:

Per day or part	£8.50
Per week	£25.50
Per month	£70.00
Per quarter	£140.00

During the period of your search you may order an abstract of any entry at a cost of £2.50. You may of course copy the details down yourself without any charge over and above the search fee.

Enquiries or orders should be addressed to:

The Registrar-General for Scotland
New Register House
Edinburgh EH1 3YT

APPENDIX II

Names and the Ancestor-hunter

Surnames or family names have in their derivations little to offer to the ancestor-hunter. They were formed perhaps five centuries before the period that most of you will be studying. In most cases of course surnames sprung up all over Britain independently of one another. And while it is of interest to, say, the bearers of the most common surname in England and Scotland to know that the first "Smith" was recorded in Durham, that fact has no genealogical significance whatsoever.

Even when a name is extremely localised—as in the case of one derived from an estate—this location will have little or no significance as a link in your own searches. My wife's family, for example, took their name from a small estate of Balbirnie in Fife. The last member of the family to own the estate had moved out before 1500, while the earliest one bearing the name which we have managed to track down was flourishing in Edinburgh around 1750. Clearly it is fanciful to draw in a long line connecting the two.

Even where the great clan names have strong territorial links, the nineteenth century knew no such limits, for by then Highlanders had spread throughout Scotland and indeed the world. Certainly one would find very many Macdonalds in the Hebrides, but equally certainly your unidentified great-grandfather Donald Macdonald could have been living anywhere in Scotland from John o'Groats to Gretna Green before he left for Canada in 1860.

And as we have seen in the book, spelling conventions have nothing like the significance we attribute to them today, so the fact that you spell your name "Miller" and not "Millar" may have no bearing whatsoever on a grandfather who may have used either spelling—or never found any need to spell it at all.

Christian names, or more correctly given names, can on the other hand prove extremely useful to the ancestor-hunter. The Scots adopted a traditional almost ritual attitude to the naming of children. Not for them the scanning of books on Boys' Names and Girls' Names when the newcomer appeared. Babies were named after relatives and the happy couple who departed from a rigid set of priorities did so at their peril and with a great risk of family friction. The list went something like this:

Sons: 1—father's father; 2—mother's father; 3—father.

Daughters: 1—mother's mother; 2—father's mother; 3—mother.

This "pecking order" as far as the naming of the new baby is concerned cannot be presented as a fixed, no-exception, formula. There were occasional regional variations, where sometimes two or even three of the people in the list bore the same name; and, sometimes, a recent death might push someone to the front of the naming queue.

Study your family's name patterns carefully, especially in the earlier years, and you will often find them giving you valuable pointers. When you come across a new name, look very hard indeed at the circumstances; it will almost certainly mean something, perhaps only the fact that a long run of boys or girls has used up the stock of traditional family Christian names.

While spelling of given names is usually more consistent than that of surnames, bear in mind that there can be variations not only in form (Ian/John, Hamish/James) but also in contractions. A Marion or an Alison may be called Mary or Ann and pass on the name to the next generation in this new form.

Today this pattern is changing and it is not so necessary to identify the many Jameses or Williams in the family by a host of additives, from Big Jimmy to Davy's Jimmie. In its place alas we have a range of strange rootless names providing variety but dissolving links.

APPENDIX III

The regularity of irregular marriages

Up until 1940, Scotland had a distinctive form of marriage, known rather imprecisely as an irregular marriage. This, the so-called Gretna Green marriage which lured panting English lovers north of the Border pursued by greybeard kinsmen brandishing swords, was a perfectly acceptable alternative to the conventional church wedding, involving instead a declaration in front of witnesses or before a sheriff. The epithet "irregular"should not lead you to believe that it was illegal or second-rate (it wasn't), or that it was indulged in by a small minority: Dr Ian Grant pointed out to me that in checking through the first 200 marriages in Glasgow Blythswood for 1904, he counted 81, more than 40 per cent, which were marriages by declaration.

By the Marriage (Scotland) Act 1939, the alternative to a church wedding became a new form of civil marriage contracted in the office and presence of certain specially authorised Registrars after publication of notice.

APPENDIX IV

Illegitimacy—a hurdle for the ancestor-hunter

A friend of mine started to tell me of a family tradition, but before mentioning any details he stopped and asked me to look into his forebears and see if I came up with anything unusual. Intrigued, I did as he asked and went speedily back three or four generations without a hiccup. Then I came across an ancestor who posed some problems which eventually boiled down to three different pairs of parents given on his marriage certificate, his death certificate and, after a long search, his birth certificate. And no one name appeared twice! No man has six parents, so I had to dream up some tale of passion, unrequited love and illegitimacy which coincided quite closely with the family tradition. My friend went one better by revealing that his family tradition held that none of the pairs were correct!

That was perhaps an extreme case of what illegitimacy can do to the ancestor-hunter. At the worst, it can bring an abrupt end to the male line or even in the case of a foundling to both lines, with little or no chance of further progress. At the mildest, it can introduce new elements into the search. It is quite common for ancestor-hunters to come across illegitimacy at some time. Just consider the following two instances as a sample of what you should bear in mind if your searches seem to be coming up against a brick wall:

1. A child might be born illegitimate and the mother might persuade the father to acknowledge paternity and give the child his name. A later separation or failure to reach the altar might mean the child reverting to the mother's name or indeed acquiring the name of her future husband. Symptom: one name on the birth certificate, a second on marriage and death certificates.

2. The mother might not be able to get the father to give his name to the child and the baptismal/birth entry would be made in the mother's name. The couple might subsequently marry and legitimise the child. Symptoms: the same as previously but with the names reversed.

APPENDIX V

Other records in New Register House

A large part of this book has been devoted to the three great treasuries of records kept by the Registrar-General for Scotland. There are, in addition to these and to the excellent array of books on the Library shelves at New Register House, other groups of records of interest to the ancestor-hunter, the first relating to events within Scotland, the others to events outside Scotland.

1. Register of Neglected entries

Births, marriages and deaths known to have occurred in Scotland between 1801 and 1854, but not included in the Old Parochial Registers.

2. Marine register of births and deaths after 1855

Births and deaths on British merchant vessels if the child's father or the deceased person was known to be Scottish. (A corresponding register exists for aircraft after 1948).

3. Service records after 1881

Births, marriages and deaths of Scottish persons serving overseas in the Armed Forces.

4. War registers from 1899

Three registers for the South African War (1899-1902), the 1914-18 War and the 1939-45 War.

5. Consular returns

Births (from 1914), marriages (from 1917) and deaths (from 1914) registered by British consuls.

6. Foreign countries

Births of children of Scottish parents, marriages and deaths of Scottish subjects, from information supplied by the parties concerned.

APPENDIX VI

Specialists in Family research

Mrs A. ROSEMARY BIGWOOD, M.A., M.Litt.
38 Primrose Bank Road, Edinburgh EH5 3JF. Tel 031-552 7980

Mrs B. A. BRACK
17 Lockharton Gardens, Edinburgh EH14 1AU. Tel 031-443 3071

Mrs DOREEN BROWN
64 Orchard Road, Edinburgh EH4 2HD. Tel 031-332 3285

DAVID BURNS
2 Bangholm Terrace, Edinburgh EH3 5QN. Tel 031-552 7340

Mrs K. B. CORY, F.S.A.Scot.
4 Brunstane Road, Joppa, Edinburgh EH15 2EY. Tel 031-669 5149

Dr B. J. IGGO, Ph.D.
5 Regulus Road, Edinburgh EH9 2NE. Tel 031-667 4879

Mrs GWEN MACLEOD
5 Bonaly Road, Edinburgh EH13 0EB. Tel 031-441 1379

Mrs S. PITCAIRN, Mem.A.G.R.A.
106 Brucefield Avenue, Dunfermline. Tel Dunfermline 25052

M. F. LLOYD PRICHARD, M.A., Ph.D.
36 Morton Street, Joppa, Edinburgh EH15 2HT. Tel 031-669 4040

SCOTTISH ROOTS
1 Castle Street, Edinburgh EH2 3AH. Tel. 031-226 2028

DANIELLA SHIPPEY, M.A.
15 Glenisla Gardens, Edinburgh EH9 2HR. Tel 031-667 4149

Ms MARGARET SINCLAIR
83 Newington Road, Edinburgh. Tel 031-667 0713

JAMES A. THOMSON
84 Gilmore Place, Edinburgh EH3 9PF. Tel 031-229 3652

APPENDIX VII

The Federation of Family History Societies

Founded in 1974 to cope with the boom in ancestor-hunters, the Federation covers the whole of Britain. A full list of societies is available from the Secretary, Mrs Ann V. Chigwell, 96 Beaumont Street, Milehouse, Plymouth, England. Here are a few of the Scottish members:

ABERDEEN & NORTH EAST SCOTLAND FHS
Miss B. J. Cowper, 31 Bloomfield Place, Aberdeen AB1 5AG.

SCOTTISH GENEALOGY SOCIETY
Miss J. Ferguson, 21 Howard Place, Edinburgh EH3 5JY.

TAY VALLEY FHS
Miss A. Pellow, c/o Messrs Carlton & Reid, Solicitors, 94 Nethergate, Dundee DD1 4EW

CARAHER FHS
Mrs D. C. Manning, Gowanlea, Willoughby Street, Muthill by Crieff, Perthshire PH5 2AB.

CLAN GAYRE ASSOCIATION
Mr D. G. Gair, 13 Regis Court, Barnton, Edinburgh EH4 6RG.

OLIVER SOCIETY
Col. W. Oliver, Blain, Blainslie, Galashiels, Selkirkshire TD1 2PR.

CLAN SUTHERLAND SOCIETY IN SCOTLAND
Dunrobin Castle, Golspie, Sutherland.

HIGHLAND FHS
Mr David Evans, 53 Ballifeary Road, Inverness.